Contents

Special Issue: Privacy II

Foreword

Concerns over privacy in America and the role of a free and responsible press have intensified in recent years. In the final two issues of 1994, the *Journal of Mass Media Ethics* has worked with the Poynter Institute for Media Studies in an effort to focus and broaden the discussion.

This issue, the second to be devoted to privacy issues, mates articles that we hope will add usefully to the current discussions of privacy issues, particularly those raised by new technology.

We take particular pride in the first article of the series, an erudite look at journalistic ethics overall as journalists approach privacy issues.

Louis Hodges, director of Washington and Lee University's center for ethics and the professions and a pioneer in professional ethics, rightly points to the very sharp conflict between a necessary right to privacy for citizens and the natural conflict of that right with the journalist's as well as society's interest in broad disclosure of information. He proposes that journalists establish their own serious tests of the public's need to know before crossing privacy invasion lines.

A lively and insightful 3-day seminar at the St. Petersburg, FL journalism "think and do tank" in December 1992 fuels the next series of contributions. The seminar brought together a group of academics, working journalists, victims' rights advocates, and newsmakers who focused on such topics as privacy and information in the computer age, private morality and public performance, revealing reality vis-à-vis violating sex crime victims, and reconciling individual rights, community values, and professional responsibilities.

Insights from some of the dozens of thoughtful participants at the Poynter Institute seminar on Privacy in America are assembled into one package for this issue. Representing those in attendance, and the general theme of the seminar, are excerpts (edited by Jay Black) by Bob Steele, Helen Benedict, Patricia Bowman, Elinor Brecher, Tom French, J. T. Johnson, Nora Paul, and Robert Ellis Smith. *JMME* is pleased to make these observations available to a wider audience.

Two of the Poynter seminar presentations are included for their unique insights into the specific emerging problems of technology and privacy. J. T. Johnson of Sartor Associates in San Francisco notes that personal information is literally scattered across a very wide geographical area while, all the same, being immediately available for a determined computer searcher wishing to assemble a "computer persona." This process, it is noted, needs no approval from the subject, nor does the subject need to be informed. Johnson says such a set of conditions calls for discussion and evaluation of existing practices.

Nora Paul, librarian at the Poynter Institute, approaches the topic from a newsroom perspective, asking whether information that is known—

developed through electronic peering—should automatically be available for publication. Her "two rights just might make a wrong" are the two that have reappeared often in these pages over the past two issues: right to know (a public and personal right) and right to privacy (a personal right). She concludes with a list of 10 specific paradoxes that need consideration by journalists confronting the issues.

Robert Ellis Smith, publisher of *Privacy Journal* and the final presenter at the Poynter conference, pulls together a number of the privacy threads: journalists' confusion over personal and public information; the right versus the need to publish; censorship vis-à-vis self-restraint. He defines privacy as "the claim of an individual to control when and where and how information about oneself is to be used," and says the problem takes on different dimensions when the subjects are public figures or officials.

Research essays on ethics in the information age appear next in this issue of the journal.

Karon Speckman, of Stephens College in Columbia, MO focuses on computer-available data bases and the problems, potential and real, of maintaining privacy when information is readily and rapidly available. She cautions about data accuracy and about using data in ways dramatically different from those intended by those who gathered them. She suggests her own guidelines for navigating this complex minefield.

Fears that such technology phenomena as audiotex are driven by techno determinism and techno imperative leads George Albert Gladney of the University of Illinois to formulate an ethical framework for its analysis. A major concern is that expansion in this field is driven more by egos than a traditional concept of community service or community good. Alarming to Gladney is a trend toward a "target model" of "giving the readers only what they want."

The case selected for our Cases and Commentaries section is of another electronic privacy sort, the distribution of information obtained from video rental records or from the public records of libraries. The privacy involved in this case is of a public official, so commentators are asked to make a moral decision in an area in which legalities for journalists are not relevant.

• • • •

A special issue of the *Journal of Mass Media Ethics* dealing with media ethics and diversity is planned for late 1995. The guest editor will be Dhyana Ziegler of the University of Tennessee–Knoxville. Contributors are invited to submit manuscripts to her at:

The University of Tennesee
Department of Broadcasting
333 Communications Building
Knoxville, TN 37996-0333
Fax: 615-974-2814
Bitnet: PA116188@UTKVM1

The Editors

Journal of Mass Media Ethics
Vol. 9, No. 4, pp. 197–212

The Journalist and Privacy

By Louis Hodges[1]
Washington and Lee University

❏*The moral right to privacy consists of the power to determine who may gain access to information about oneself. Individual human beings need some measure of privacy in order to develop a sense of self and to avoid manipulation by the state. Journalists who respect the privacy rights of those on whom they report should especially be careful not to intrude unduly when gathering information; in publishing they should be able to demonstrate a public need to know private information. Individual journalists should establish their own guidelines for reporting on the private lives of different categories of people in the news.*

Privacy is an issue of unparalleled importance in this decade. The ability of government, corporations, and journalists to invade the lives of private citizens has dramatically increased through the advent of ever more sensitive listening devices, chemical drug tests, credit files, and widely distributed medical files. Hungry business organizations send people such things as mail-order catalogues and credit card offers that are generated by sophisticated use of data from records of what they buy in stores.

As our ability to invade privacy has increased, so too has our willingness to do so. Witness *USA Today*'s probing into Arthur Ashe's illness, mainline media revealing Patricia Bowman's identity as William Kennedy Smith's rape accuser, or even Senate demands for the private diaries of Senator Bob Packwood. Each of these cases involves public intrusion into private matters as well as revelation of private information in the public forum. How can we decide, and by what criteria, when an invasion of privacy is morally justified?

Totally apart from questions of ethics, the issue of privacy has become significant for the press in terms of its own self-interest, a matter of prudence. Though many people show interest in private information about others, many others are offended by journalists' conduct, and that has led to increased distrust of the press. When we see reporters poking microphones into the face of a mother who has just witnessed a fire that killed her three children, most of us are morally outraged. (It is interesting that we witness such behavior because other photographers show their fellow journalists in action!) Is it surprising that journalists enjoy low public esteem?

Consider again the Arthur Ashe case, this time as an example of the invasion of privacy and the public response (American Press Institute, 1992). Having won at Wimbledon and in the U.S. Open, Ashe in the 1970s was ranked No. 1 in the tennis world. After brain surgery in 1988, he learned that he was infected with HIV, the virus that causes AIDS, as a result of a blood transfusion in 1983. Many of his friends, including a number of reporters, knew of his condition and kept his secret. But in 1993 *USA Today* sent a reporter to ask Ashe about his having the virus. Ashe did not answer the question but was told that the newspaper would pursue the story. Although he had wanted to make his own statement later in his own way and at a time of his own choosing, Ashe called a news conference the next day and announced to the world, against his will, that he had AIDS. Gene Policinski, sports editor for *USA Today,* with the support of senior executives, offered the lame excuse: "The news was that one of the great athletes of this century had a fatal illness—and that the illness was AIDS. By any journalist's definition, that's news" (Policinski, 1992, p. 17).

Public response to what *USA Today* did to Ashe was strongly negative, as was the response of responsible journalists all over the country. Most people who have had things to say about the newspaper's moral irresponsibility and insensitivity to Ashe's interests would acknowledge the paper's legal right to do what it did. The concern was over the absence of a moral right to do what was perfectly legal. It is the moral concern, not the legal, that I write about here.

In what follows, I propose to inquire into the nature of privacy in human affairs, the need for it, and the right to it. A fourth section inquires into the need for privacy in relation to the need of people to know, that is, competing needs that give rise to competing rights. Finally, I suggest some moral guidelines that journalists might consider in reporting on the private lives of several categories of people.

The Nature of Privacy

To think about the ethics of privacy, one must begin by examining the meaning of the word. Bok (1982) defines privacy as "the condition of being protected from unwanted access by others—either physical access, personal information, or attention" (pp. 10–11). Westin (1967) identified privacy with "the claim of individuals, groups, or institutions to determine for themselves when, how, and to what extent information about them is communicated to others" (p. 7).

Levine (1980) shared some of Westin's language but expanded the definition slightly when he wrote: "[Privacy] is the maintenance of a personal life-space within which the individual has a chance to be an individual, to exercise and experience his own uniqueness" (p. 19).

Similar themes appeared in Breckenridge (1980):

> Privacy, in my view, is the rightful claim of the individual to determine the extent to which he wishes to share of himself with others and his control over the time, place, and circumstances to communicate to others. It means his right

to withdraw or to participate as he sees fit. It is also the individual's right to control dissemination of information about himself; it is his own personal possession. (p. 1)

Perhaps Cooley (1888) put it most succinctly when he identified privacy as "the right to be let alone" (p. 29).

The language I prefer comes from Westin. He says about privacy:

The claim is not so much one of total secrecy as it is of the right to define one's circle of intimacy—to choose who shall see beneath the quotidian mask. Loss of control over which "face" one puts on may result in literal loss of self-identity. (as quoted in *Dietemann v. Time, Inc.*, 1971)

The visual image of a "circle of intimacy" is helpful for an understanding of what is meant by privacy. It invites us to imagine ourselves standing at the center of a series of concentric circles of intimacy in which the degree of intimacy diminishes from the innermost circle outward.

In the innermost circle you are alone. Some things about yourself you and you alone know—fantasies, unarticulated hopes, memories—and you would feel violated and invaded if someone learned those things against your will. You occupy the second circle with at least one other person, perhaps a spouse, sometimes a professional, such as a member of the clergy, a lawyer, a doctor, or a college counselor. In this second circle you share intimacies that you want only the one other person to know. You reveal yourself, your innermost being. With your spouse the revelations are, or should be if the relationship is to endure, reciprocal. If the other is your doctor or your counselor or your minister, the revelation is largely unidirectional. The point is that in this second circle you are in the primary private relation with one other human being. The bond is fiduciary. The relationship rests on trust, trust that the one to whom you have revealed yourself will neither betray the trust nor use the revelation to your disadvantage. Our law recognizes the importance of these primary relationships by not requiring spouses to testify against each other and by protecting the lawyer–client relationship.

The third circle from center contains others to whom you are very close. Under one circumstance it may include your family. It might incorporate close friends, fellow fraternity or sorority members, athletic or debate teammates. Whoever is in this circle with you comes to know things about you that you would not want to be public knowledge. You reveal some of your peculiarities—your flaws, your dreams—because you are confident that the people in this circle will not use that information to your detriment.

One can extend this image of circles to the outermost imaginable circle, the least intimate, which encompasses all humanity. There are some things about yourself that you would not object to all humanity knowing. Those things constitute your most public self.

In terms of this picture, to have privacy is to possess control over your circles of intimacy, to determine who enters each one and who does not. You may choose to be a very private person, bent on concealing yourself, or you may be very public, willing to share intimacies widely with others. Whichever you choose to be, the important issue morally is your right to decide just how public or private you will be.

The Need for Privacy

Most people acknowledge the desire for privacy, the desire to control access to their circles of intimacy. We seem to know instinctively the importance of privacy for civilized existence. But can our desire for privacy be related to a real human need? Yes. Privacy plays a central role in human affairs. Without some degree of privacy, civilized life would not be possible. The ability to control access to our circles of intimacy meets any number of basic human needs, but the two that seem uppermost are psychological and political.

The Psychological Need

Psychologically speaking, privacy is a precondition for developing a sense of self, an awareness of the boundaries between the self and others. Fischer (1980) used Erik Erikson's description of the stages of human development from infancy to maturity. People need private relations, she noted, in order to "try out" new poses—future selves—without fear of ridiculing intrusion by others. Privacy provides the opportunity to imagine possible futures without commitment to any until several have been projected. It provides opportunities to examine fantasies, dreams, hopes, and so forth, through intimate interaction with trusted others. Privacy shields against the stifling effect of convention. In that way it protects the emerging, still-disordered self while simultaneously allowing for the continuation of custom and convention that are so essential for social order.

In other words, control over our circles of intimacy is necessary if we are to have some control over who we are, over what kind of person we are and wish to become. It gives us a chance to develop our own particular identity, that unique self-consciousness that sets us up as distinct from, but always a part of, the world and the larger mass of humanity. The human need for privacy seems self-evident to anyone who imagines what it would be like never to be alone, never to entertain a private thought or perform a private act. George Orwell's (1949) *1984* is a sufficient reminder!

The psychological need for privacy is recognized in the law as well. Blaustein (1964), for example, noted that "our law of privacy attempts to preserve individuality by placing sanctions upon outrageous or unreasonable violation of the conditions for its sustenance." Without it, he added, "an individual merges with the mass" (p. 962).

The Political Need

Orwell (1949) pointed also to the need for privacy as a shield against the power of the state. The more one knows about a person the easier it is to influence, manipulate, or even control him or her. In fact, some scholars argue that liberal democracy is unthinkable without effective guarantees of privacy. Neville (1980) put it this way:

> Precisely because the state is seen as the agency of the citizen's own authority, its independent power is feared, and limitations on the power of the state, such as the Bill of Rights, were established in order to protect private life. Privacy then comes to be viewed as that area of personal life in which the state should make no claim, at least not without due process designed to protect privacy. One of the strong connotations of privacy today is the negative sense that it is where others have no right to intrude. (p. 25)

In this negative sense—freedom from government control—privacy is central to the liberal democratic ideal. Historically, totalitarian societies have used high visibility—the near absence of privacy—as a major ingredient in their drive to produce a homogeneous and servile populace. As Dionisopoulos and Ducat (1976) noted:

> Nor is it any mere coincidence that accounts for the fact that, in a free democratic society, public affairs are usually marked by openness and private affairs are normally shielded from view, while, in totalitarian states, the reverse is generally true.[2] (p. 4)

Liberal democracy employs privacy as a check on the state. That fact is based on the recognition that to have knowledge about a person is to hold power over that person. One who has no privacy, one who is completely open, is readily coerced. Politically speaking, privacy represents the power to control access to one's self, and, thus, it conveys some capacity to resist the coercive power of the state.

Thus, it seems clear that, because privacy is essential to meeting basic psychological and political needs, it must not be taken lightly. Indeed, privacy lies at the very heart of the most cherished values of Western civilization: freedom, the dignity of humankind, and individual autonomy. Believing as we do in the basic right and duty of individual human beings to work out their destinies in community with others, our civilization developed ways of protecting privacy. As another writer stated:

> With increasing attention to, and recognition of, human dignity in Western society in recent centuries and particularly in recent years, there has come a parallel emphasis on human rights, and central to the cluster of human rights is the right to privacy. (Bier, 1980, p. x)

We may now turn our attention from the need for and importance of privacy to the question of a right to privacy.

The Right to Privacy

Surprisingly, articulated claims to a right to privacy do not go far back in history. No specific right to privacy is guaranteed by the Bill of Rights, though it is reasonable to claim that privacy is assumed as necessary to the guarantee of other rights. In the law, tort claims based specifically on the right to privacy began to be recognized only in this century. The now-famous law review article by Warren and Brandeis (1890) is widely credited with precipitating 20th-century law of privacy. It was the law review article that launched a tort.

Though the law of privacy is both important and expanding, it is not of concern here. I am concerned, rather, with the more fundamental issue of privacy as a moral right to control the entrance of others into one's circles of intimacy. Moral discourse always has a certain primacy over legal discourse, so moral discourse must always precede the making of laws if laws are to be wisely made.

The claim of a moral right to privacy grows ultimately out of certain observations about the very nature of the human being. Individually we are unique entities possessing our own personal identities, memories, hopes, and goals. Thus, individuals need to identify the boundaries, physical and spiritual, that set them apart as separate entities. We are in part autonomous beings, self-ruling, self-directing. Because privacy, defined as control over access to one's circles of intimacy, is essential to self-identity and self-direction, people assert privacy as a right.

But the right to privacy is not absolute. It stands beside a countervailing right of others to know quite a lot about us as individuals. These two legitimate rights—the individual right to a measure of privacy and the right of others to know some things about the individual—frame the moral issues.

Just as the claim to a right to privacy grows out of some observations about human nature and human need, so does the claim to a right to know about others. Because we are individual beings, we have a need (right) for privacy; because we are social beings, we have a need (right) to know. People especially need to know quite a lot about those who have power over them. Paradoxically, people's very images of themselves are shaped in quite large measures by the way others perceive them, so for that reason we need to know just how they perceive us. Moreover, our sense of individual purpose and destiny is inextricably tied to the fortunes, purposes, and destinies of others. What they do has effects on us and we on them. These observations may be summed up this way: Because humans are individual beings, the total elimination of privacy would eliminate human existence as we know it; because we are social beings, the elevation of privacy to absolute status would likewise render human existence impossible.

These claims to competing rights, taken together, frame the moral problem: Just when, in specific cases, should civil societies allow intrusion on private affairs, and under what conditions should they forbid it? Where should society draw the moral line between society's need (and right) to know and the individual's need (and right) not to reveal? More specifically, what should the responsible journalist take into account in drawing that line while gathering and disseminating information?

Reporting and Privacy

The privacy issue arises at two points in the reporting process. The first is at the point of gathering information, where decisions have to be made about *intrusion* by the journalist into the lives of subjects. The second is at the point of deciding what to publish, where decisions are made about what private facts are appropriate for *dissemination*. Journalists at the second point are positioned to determine for the subject what circle of intimacy the public may enter.

Whether journalists are concerned about gathering or disseminating, the general questions are these: Under what conditions is a journalist justified in gathering and reporting information about a person against that person's will? Where should reporters and editors draw the line between the private and the public self? What in specific cases justifies an invasion of individual privacy by journalists? When is it just to override an individual's right to privacy for the public good?

I suggest the following as the formal criterion: It is just for a journalist to violate the privacy of an individual only if information about that individual is of overriding public importance and the public need cannot be met by other means. As a formal criterion, of course, this does not tell us what information to publish in specific cases, but it does provide a test for any particular decision on privacy.

Note that this criterion does not permit invasion of privacy to obtain and publish information that the public is interested in but that is not important for the public to know. The mere fact that the public is curious about private information or conduct ordinarily is not sufficient reason to obtain and publish it against the will of the person reported on.

"Curiosity" is the psychological ground of many of our "interests." Most of us have a kind of healthy curiosity, or inquisitiveness, about the world around us. But we also are capable of such things as morbid curiosity and prurient interest. Clearly, the latter two are not grounds for invading someone's privacy, though they are the criteria that gossip sheets use. But even the healthy form of curiosity, where the public is legitimately interested in a story, should not be allowed to override an individual's right to privacy. That is simply because no genuine need would be served.

The mere fact that people want to know is not enough to warrant the harm done to an individual by an invasion of his or her circles of intimacy. Any significant harm to the individual outweighs the public benefit in every imaginable case. To deny a person control over his or her circles of intimacy is to deny that person a measure of dignity. Loss of control of intimacy poses a threat to one's sense of self. It deprives one of a measure of control over oneself. Better that the public be deprived of an interesting story than that journalists harm the individual about whom that story could be written. There are enough interesting stories about interesting people, which we can publish with their permission, without hearing about those who do not want to be in the news. On those grounds the principle of overriding public importance would rule out "interest" as a sufficient test.

But what would that principle allow? How might reporters and editors determine, in particular cases, what is and what is not important enough to justify an invasion of privacy? It is not possible, of course, to establish rules that are narrow enough to determine specific cases in ways that eliminate the need for careful thought. But it is possible to state some general criteria, or tests, that can guide the journalist through decisions and help test them. After all, journalists on a daily basis make judgments about the relative importance of stories.

Let us begin the search for criteria by asking what it means for a story to be important. Stories contain both information and ideas. From information and ideas people acquire knowledge that they can use in living. It follows logically that the relative importance of specific bits of knowledge can be determined only by judgments about what people need to live well in their specific environment and in their different roles—citizen, parent, worker, consumer, and so forth. What people need in order to function in those roles is ordinarily quite obvious, at least at both ends of the continuum. At one end some knowledge is clearly indispensable. For example, if citizens are to vote sensibly, they must have knowledge of what governments are doing and not doing. At the other end of the continuum of relative importance, it is of no relevance whatsoever that citizens know which of the President's knees grows the warts. In the midsection of the continuum, however, judgments about importance of information are not so obvious. They require careful thought and examination, using the question: Will this information help citizens make their own decisions more wisely? Is this "news they can use?"

Some knowledge, of course, is important because of its intrinsic value—its value as an important end in itself—that is, self-knowledge. Other knowledge is important only extrinsically—valuable only as a means to some end—that is, that Route 60 leads west to Kerrs Creek. Journalists qua journalists are seldom, if ever, called upon to deal with intrinsically valuable knowledge. Perhaps a story about a person courageously confronting adversity would qualify, because it calls reader's attention to the human condition. But ordinarily the knowledge readers can gain from news columns is only extrinsically valuable: The information in news columns is important only if it can lead to knowledge the public needs in order to function well. A story, to follow this logic, is important insofar as the use to which it might be put is important. For instance, a story about the dangers of kerosene heaters is important because it enables people to use those heaters carefully or not at all. A story about a Caribbean cruise is important because it can help people plan a vacation. Moreover, the story about the heaters is more important than the one about the cruise. Why? Because saving a life is more important than taking a vacation. And such judgments are easy to make because sensible people agree most of the time on the relative importance of most things.

So, the test of importance calls for judgments about what people need to know in order to live well. Invasions of privacy, in this scheme of things, are justified only when the public's need to know private things about an individual is strong enough to override that individual's need for and moral right to privacy.

So far I have proposed the general principle of overriding public importance as a general criterion. It remains to suggest how that principle might function when applied to particular cases and classes of cases. No doubt conscientious people will disagree in the particulars, even if they accept the criterion in principle. What follows is an attempt at guidelines for several categories of people in the news.

Some Guidelines on Privacy

Public Officials

In reporting on public officials we should publish private information, even against their will, if their private activity might reasonably have a significant effect on their official performance.

It is of overwhelming importance in a democracy that the people know what their governors are doing. That knowledge is essential for responsible citizenship. The higher ranking the official, the more power that person has to improve or wreck lives. Thus, it is in the public interest to know anything about those officials that might affect their wielding of power or their discharge of the public trust. And that can include almost everything—health, leisure activities, marital condition, personal taste, and countless other subjects. But there are limits even for the highest ranking officials. The story must pass the test of having significance for the official's capacity or willingness to perform official duties.

In a democratic state, citizens have reason to want the lives of officials open to public scrutiny. Openness is essential if the public is to hold them accountable, and public people usually know that most of their privacy is lost once they enter public life. For instance, consider the case of presidential hemorrhoids. Ordinarily, it is of no public significance that some poor soul suffers from that ailment. But in the case of the President of the United States, even that becomes important news: We do not want him in pain while he is making foreign policy decisions. Also, when the President visits the hospital, it is important that the public know why, that the visit was for hemorrhoids and not a brain tumor. Similarly, the sexual activities of a senator would usually not be of importance to citizens, but when he puts his paramour on the public payroll it becomes important.

Lately, much has been made over extramarital sexual behavior by such high officials as Senator Bob Packwood (R-Oregon) and former Senator Brock Adams (D-Washington). There is concern over marital infidelity and over sexual harassment. Because private sexual activity between consenting adults, even outside marriage, poses little or no threat to performance of public duty, that activity is not a legitimate public concern under our standard. Therefore, it has no place in legitimate news. Sexual harassment, however, is quite another matter. The one being harassed gives no consent and is typically the victim of abuse of power. It is important to readers to know about harassment, but usually not about mere infidelity.

Public Figures

In reporting on public figures, we should publish private information, even against their will, if their private activity might significantly affect their performance of duties to their publics.

The public figure category includes top officials in private organizations, including senior executives in industry, business, labor, education, philanthropic organizations, and the like. News about them is important because of the power and authority they wield over others, both within and outside their own organizations. What is good for General Motors may or may not be good for the country, but it surely affects the country. For example, questions of health and medical condition, which are private matters for most citizens, are of legitimate public concern insofar as they could have significant effect on performance.

The public needs to know about those individuals who sit in private seats of power, because power can corrupt, whether in the public or the private sector. It is because of their power that public figures are more than merely interesting.

Just as for public officials, the test of importance would not justify publishing everything we can get about public figures. Some privacy should be preserved. It is difficult to imagine, for example, why the public would need to know of an executive's enjoyment of gay or lesbian rather than heterosexual companions. How could that orientation significantly affect job performance? In general, however, in reporting on the privately powerful a bias toward openness rather than privacy and secrecy is warranted, and the greater their power, the lower their threshold of privacy.

Celebrities

We should publish private information about them if readers are interested in knowing that information, provided that the information does no harm to the celebrity as a person. (The criterion of "interest" surpasses that of "importance.")

Under the law, celebrities are public figures, but morally they are different. Jack Smith, Chief Executive Officer of General Motors, is important because of his power to rule, to govern the lives of thousands. John Wayne was important because of his influence as a role model.

By "celebrities," I mean such categories as movie stars, television personalities, ball players, and the like. On the one hand, they surely have some right to privacy. On the other hand, their professional life succeeds or fails depending on their ability to become public. Their admirers are "fans" in part because of the kind of people they are, and fans want to know what the celebrity is like in real life. By their choice of occupation or social function, essentially entertainment, celebrities must waive all but the narrowest measure of privacy.

Warren Beatty (1983) states the case fairly succinctly:

> Privacy is a sort of simple matter in my case. I don't have any, and I don't really expect any.
> I knew what business I was going into when I went into the movies, and I think probably there is something in all of us that would be sort of disappointed to be left alone. (p. A-10)

Carol Burnett (1983) echoes some of the same:

> A public figure has little in the way of private life. That's a fact of life for those involved in careers that increase public visibility; with increased visibility comes natural curiosity to know more about the person.
> That the public feels a kind of intimacy with familiar figures is certainly understandable. Once an individual has achieved public recognition—almost always accomplished through willing participation—it is a journalist's prerogative to report information that he or she feels the public is interested in, or should know.
> It's also the journalist's responsibility to make certain what is reported is correct. . . . Someone said that if you don't want something quoted, don't say it, and if you don't want something reported, don't do it. The injury is done in quoting what wasn't said, or in reporting what wasn't done. (p. A-10)

People like Beatty and Burnett are thus willing, or at least resigned, to sacrifice a significant measure of privacy for other rewards. Even so, although it is interesting to know about the private doings of celebrities, it is not very important in the larger scheme of things. It is important, however, that journalists do celebrities no harm by reporting conditions over which they have no control. The Arthur Ashe AIDS story is a case in point. So, beyond the harm principle, the moral criteria seem to be "interest" and "accuracy." These are usually interesting people, and as human beings we need interesting stories about interesting people. And there is nothing wrong with being interested in them. They can add a measure of spice to life's sometimes drab menu.

Temporarily Newsworthy Heroes

In reporting on people who have performed heroic acts, we should publish only that private information that relates directly to the newsworthy act.

Common citizens from time to time do things, usually acts of heroism, that for a moment put them in the limelight. Consider the case of Oliver Sipple (Elliott & Linsky, 1982). On September 22, 1975, Sipple deflected the gun that Sarah Jane Moore fired at President Gerald Ford, thus probably saving his life. Because of his heroic act it is both important and interesting that we know something about Sipple, where he came from, what he does, whether anything in his background helped him know how to deflect the gun or to generate the reflexes to do it. It was relevant, for example, that he was a former Marine. But it was not important to know personal matters not related to the action that made him a momentary hero. The fact of his gay orientation, which he did not want generally known and which his family did not know, was clearly not relevant to his action, so there was no overriding public need that would justify publishing that fact of his private life. Positive harm was done by publication of information about his gay orientation when his family abandoned him.

Thus, in the case of the temporarily newsworthy hero I suggest the guideline of publishing only that private information related directly to the newsworthy act itself. That person should have the moral right to keep everything else private if he or she wishes.

Criminals

In reporting on criminal behavior we should report all aspects of the criminal's private life that might help to understand the criminal and his or her acts.

Society needs to have the clearest understanding of criminal behavior and of the criminal mind. The more severe the crime, that is, the more damaging the crime to individuals and society, the more justified we are in probing the criminal's private life for clues that contribute to an understanding of the person, not merely of his or her criminal act. One might also reasonably argue that a person who has chosen to commit a criminal act has by that choice given up rights that society normally confers. Should the right to privacy be among them? Yes, insofar as probing into the criminal's private affairs may help society in dealing with criminal conduct. Thus, the journalistic bias should be in the direction of openness and revelation rather than secrecy and privacy.

On this point, however, a special word of caution is in order. An accused person is not a criminal until he or she has been tried and convicted. This guideline should not apply to people merely suspected of crime, not even those already arrested and bound for trial. Moreover, pretrial publicity can be seriously damaging to due process and fair trial, and for that reason editorial judgments must be made with special caution. To probe the private life of mere suspects risks serious damage to innocent people. A just society still presumes innocence until guilt is proven.

Innocent Victims of Crime and Tragedy

We should report about them only that which they give permission to publish.

This is a special category of people with special needs and vulnerability who are frequently treated badly by the press. In a Virginia hamlet, for example, a policeman was killed in the line of duty. The community, and many nearby communities, were much bestirred by the shooting. The media gave the entire affair extensive coverage. On the day of the slain officer's funeral an area television news crew showed up at the cemetery and with a long-distance lens filmed, and subsequently broadcast, the grieving widow leaving the cemetery. The reporters did not know whether she minded being seen on the news in the state of grief. It seems arguable that if she wanted to work out her tears in the privacy and warmth of family and friends, she should have every right to do so. She should have the right to choose not to appear on television. The public, though perhaps interested, had nothing important to gain by observing her under those conditions.

Likewise, there is no public good to come from the frequent journalistic (mostly television) practice of dispatching a reporter to a burning house to film and interview the owner/victim. The burning house, the cause and extent of the fire, the danger of wood stoves, the leaking gas line are publicly important, but not the private grief of the owner. In these cases, moreover, it is possible to tell the important story of tragedy without interviewing or filming the victim. If the victim does not want to talk to the news media, the journalist who insists places an added burden on that victim. If the victim is filmed against his or her will, the victim has lost yet more control of his or her life than the loss occasioned by the fire. That loss is not balanced by a public gain. The victim's privacy should not be violated. The victim has a right to be let alone.

Among the most hotly debated examples of reporting on victims are those involving rape and sexual molestation (Lake, 1991). It is unfortunate, but nevertheless true, that a social stigma still attaches to victims of rape. That is largely because many people continue to think of rape as a sex crime when it is in fact a particularly heinous form of violent crime. Rape victims who are identified in the media ordinarily suffer the consequences of the stigma, thus adding to the harm already caused by the rape itself. Another moral concern is the effect of public identification upon victims' willingness to report actual rape. Victims who would not only have to endure a public trial but also receive media publicity are discouraged from reporting the fact that they had been raped. For these reasons nearly all news organizations have policies against identifying victims without their consent (Overholser, 1989).

A few organizations, however, always identify. They usually make two arguments in favor of doing so. First, they believe that reporting victims' names will help overcome the social stigma (Sanders, 1980). Such thinking is seriously flawed, however, because there are better ways of fighting the stigma (i.e., reporting on the crime of rape and using names of only those victims who give consent). Also, to report victims' names for that reason is to use individuals as mere means to others' ends, which violates one of the basic moral rules. Second, organizations that identify rape victims sometimes argue that out of fairness reporters should reveal the accuser/victim if the accused/perpetrator is revealed. That thinking too is flawed because there is a good reason for identifying the accused that does not apply to the accuser: People need to know about arrests so as to keep watch on police.

For all these reasons, I conclude that rape victims should not be identified in news reports without their consent. Sufficient numbers of them will consent, and reporting on those who do will gradually erode the stigma.

Adult Relatives of the Prominent

We should report on them only because of the significance of what they do, not because of their family ties.

Relatives of the prominent are often treated differently from the rest of us. Why? One argument is that all members of a close family derive social benefits precisely because of a prominent relative. Therefore, they should also bear the burdens of prominence. That argument rests on some theory of just allocation of benefits and burdens. What it does not consider is the damaging effect of publicity on the prominent person who had no control over the conduct of the relative. The President, for example, should neither be harmed by nor benefit from whatever his "long-lost brother" did or does.

Although it is not important that the public be told about relatives, they are nevertheless of interest to the public. Is that adequate justification for making the families public against their will? Arguably not. If they have not sought prominence, and if they wish to be let alone, they should be. Like other citizens, they should be reported on because of the significance of what they do, not because of family ties to the prominent. If they want to remain behind the scenes, they should be allowed to do so.

There is a circumstance, however, in which relatives of the prominent give up much of their right to privacy. For example, some years ago, Senator Ted Kennedy, a candidate for reelection, had made every effort to use his wife Joan as a major political asset. She was shown in the campaign as a devoted wife, loving mother, and constant companion, a person much to be admired. During the campaign, however, she had a traffic accident, apparently while under the influence, and smashed a car or two. The wreck, ordinarily not newsworthy, was reported by Roger Mudd on *CBS News*. Mudd (speaking to a class at Washington and Lee University) reasoned that because she had been shown as an asset to her husband, she was newsworthy when she became a liability, and that justified broadcast of news about a rather unspectacular traffic accident. Because the Senator had tried to persuade people to vote for him because of her, he made her a public figure. That changes the applicable guidelines.

The reader might well refine and extend this list. I present it merely as a sample designed to show that it is possible to state some defensible guidelines that can help journalists decide when to invade (and when not to invade) the privacy of people under different circumstances. Most journalists have norms, but they are rarely articulated. They should be stated so that journalists may more effectively examine and evaluate their own norms.

Summary and Conclusion

One who possesses privacy possesses control over the entrance of others into his or her circles of intimacy. The possession of privacy is of utmost importance to individuals and societies for psychological reasons (need for individual identity and autonomy) and for political reasons (to curtail the power of the state). But morally speaking, the right to privacy must be limited by recognition of the need of others to know about individuals. Thus, in reporting on individuals journalists should temper invasions of privacy in particular cases by applying the test of the public's real need to know.

Notes

1. This article will appear as a chapter in a forthcoming book by Louis W. Hodges and John C. Merrill: *Ethical Foundations for Journalists: Toward a Sound Professional Life* (Harcourt Brace, 1995).
2. The link between privacy and the liberal ideal is explored also in Fuller (1969) and Polanyi (1951).

References

American Press Institute. (1992). *The public, privacy, and the press*. Reston, VA: Author.

Beatty, W. (1983, May 16). Press must get tough on its own abuses. *USA Today*, p. A-10.

Bier, W. (1980). *Privacy: A vanishing value?* New York: Fordham University Press.

Blaustein, E. (1964). Privacy as an aspect of human dignity: An answer to Dean Prosser. *New York University Law Review, 39*, 962–1007.

Bok, S. (1982). *Secrets: On the ethics of concealment and revelation.* New York: Pantheon.

Breckenridge, A. (1980). *The right to privacy.* Lincoln: University of Nebraska Press.

Burnett, C. (1983, May 16). Once printed, words have nine lives. *USA Today*, p. A-10.

Cooley, T. (1888). *A treatise on the law of torts* (2nd ed.). Chicago: Callaghan.

Dietemann v. Time, Inc., 449 F. 2d 245 (1971).

Dionisopoulos, P., & Ducat, C. (1976). *The right to privacy: Essays and cases.* St. Paul, MN: West.

Elliott, D., & Linsky, M. (1982, September). The Oliver Sipple story: The questions it raises for the press. *The Bulletin of the American Society of Newspaper Editor*, p. 1

Fischer, C. (1980). Privacy and human development. In W. Bier (Ed.), *Privacy: A vanishing value?* (pp. 35–37). New York: Fordham University Press.

Fuller, L. (1969). *The morality of law.* New Haven, CT: Yale University Press.

Lake, J. (1991). Of crime and consequence: Should newspapers report rape complainants' names? *Journal of Mass Media Ethics, 6,* 106–118.

Levine, M. (1980). Privacy in the tradition of the Western world. In W. Bier (Ed.), *Privacy: A vanishing value?* (pp. 3–21). New York: Fordham University Press.

Neville, R. (1980). Various meanings of privacy: A philosophical analysis. In W. Bier (Ed.), *Privacy: A vanishing value?* (pp. 22–23). New York: Fordham University Press.

Orwell, G. (1949). *1984: A novel.* New York: Harcourt, Brace.

Overholser, G. (1989, November). We should not have to keep hiding rape. *The Bulletin of the American Society of Newspaper Editors*, p. 32.

Polanyi, M. (1951). *The logic of liberty.* Chicago: University of Chicago Press.

Policinski, G. (1992, July/August). The Arthur Ashe AIDS story is news. *The Bulletin of the American Society of Newspaper Editors*, p. 17.

Sanders, W. (1980). *Rape and woman's identity.* Beverly Hills, CA: Sage.

Warren, S., & Brandeis, L. (1890). The right to privacy. *Harvard Law Review, 4*(5), 193–220.

Westin, A. (1967). *Privacy and freedom.* New York: Atheneum.

Journal of Mass Media Ethics
Vol. 9, No. 4, pp. 213–234

Privacy in America: The Frontier of Duty and Restraint

Edited by Jay Black

❑*Topics at a Poynter Institute privacy conference in December 1992 ranged from the role and obligations of the journalist to the rights of victims. Journalists' responsibility to fulfill a dual role of truthtelling and minimizing harm to vulnerable people in society framed the discussion. The public's curiosity and media obsessions with information about victims of sex crimes are the first topics to be explored. Bob Steele of the Poynter Institute sets the stage for the delicate balance. Helen Benedict, author of* Virgin or Vamp: How the Press Covers Sex Crimes, *suggests some reforms regarding this area of news. Patricia Bowman, a victim's advocate, talks about her experience as the victim of the media and of a celebrated sex crime case. Elinor Brecher of the* Miami Herald *discusses a particularly vexing assignment she recently faced, and* Tom French of the St. Petersburg Times *expresses concern for the subjects of sensitive personal stories and recommends trying to inform them about the story and help them cope with the intrusion into their private life.*

In separate articles, J. T. Johnson of Sartor Associates in San Francisco and Nora Paul of the Poynter Institute offer insights into the paradox of individual privacy and public right/desire to know, particularly as the issues arise in today's information society. Finally, Robert Ellis Smith, publisher of Privacy *Journal, outlines ways media can approach privacy issues and still feel they are on safe ground; he recommends self-restraint in place of government restrictions.*

The general theme of the Poynter Conference is restraint—and concern for others—responsible usage of information that has the possibility to harm others.

Editors' Note:

The following are excerpts from the discussion on privacy issues covered at the Poynter Institute for Media Studies "Privacy in America" conference at the St. Petersburg, FL journalism "think and do tank" in December 1992.

In the months following that conference, major news stories and dramatic changes in the information superhighway's capacity to focus attention on individuals have given rise to still more questions about what has been called "the right to be let alone," or an individual's right to control when and how information about him or her will be disclosed. Much has been written and said lately about the increasing difficulties faced by journalists who hope to responsibly cover significant news events without unnecessarily prying into private lives. As noted elsewhere on the pages of this issue of *JMME*, and in the previous issue, the task becomes ever more difficult in a climate of tabloid journalism and techno-wizardry.

Consider what Marvin Kalb had to say in an October 10, 1994 column syndicated by the *Los Angeles Times*. Kalb, chief diplomatic correspondent for CBS and NBC, is serving as a visiting professor of press and public policy at George Washington University, where he has thoughtfully taken stock of some recent media trends:

> Now, nothing is what it seems. Suddenly, after radical changes in technology and journalistic norms, there is a disturbing blurring of the line between news and entertainment, between reporting and editorializing, between fact and opinion, between "old" and "new" media—between [Ted] Koppel and [Larry] King. The result is confusion in the news room and the living room.
>
> CBS anchor Walter Cronkite used to be enough—"the most trusted man in America," he was called. But now, bewilderingly, there are hundreds of sources—from traditional news shows to call-in talk shows, from electronic town meetings to faxes, 800– and 900–numbers and on-line bulletin boards, from Capitol Gang and Meet the Press to religion programs that mix faith with politics.
>
> Add to this the avalanche of information newspapers and tabloids, magazines and newsletters. You can see that the difficulty of distinguishing real from fake has become almost insurmountable. "News" may be news, but it may also be gossip, half-truth, outlandish fiction, scandal or sensational and unsubstantiated tidbits, masquerading as "news." News is no longer an easily definable commodity.

At a time when media and the public have grown confused over triviality and significance—a mediafest lunching on O. J. Simpson, Michael Jackson, Tonya Harding and Nancy Kerrigan, the Menendez brothers, Amy Fisher and the like—Kalb considers the problems caused by blurring of news and talk shows, traditional news values competing with tabloid values, and, audiences that believe they are getting news from *Hard Copy* and *Rescue 911*. He questions whether journalism can ever recover its former authority. His answer: "Perhaps—but it will require a monumental struggle, and the outcome is far from assured. . . . What is needed is a new commitment to honest, old-fashioned journalism—and to courage."

That commitment to time-honored traditions of truthtelling and courageous reporting, coupled with sensitivity toward news sources and a commitment to "public journalism" and a renewed sense of civics, provided the framework for discussions at the Poynter Institute seminar on Privacy in America. Following are insights from some of the dozens of thoughtful participants at that conference. *JMME* is pleased to make these observations available to a wider audience.

The following is a departure from the usual style and format followed by JMME, *in order that the information could be presented in a way that would give the feeling and essence of the more informal delivery method of the conference.*

Bob Steele
Director of Ethics Programs, Poynter Institute for Media Studies

Excellent journalism and concern for privacy are not mutually exclusive goals. Nobody else has the same information gathering and disseminating professional obligation that journalism has, and if journalists do not do it, nobody will. I am a strong believer in the obligation of journalism to do its very best to seek out the truth and to report it, to portray events and issues as best as possible, even when the revelations of

> *"Excellent journalism and concern for privacy are not mutually exclusive goals."*
> —Bob Steele

words and sounds and pictures and images cause some harm.

I believe journalists should begin with the assumption, the obligation really, that information is to be published or broadcast, unless there is a compelling and overriding reason to the contrary, and that should be rare. To be sure, I also believe that journalists should have the ethical decision-making capacity to choose alternatives to fulfill both principles: truthtelling and minimizing harm to those who are vulnerable. Good ethical decision-making helps minimize harm.

Helen Benedict
Journalism Professor, Columbia University,
and Author, *Virgin or Vamp: How the Press Covers Sex Crimes*
(New York: Oxford University Press, 1992)

Privacy is at the bottom of every controversy that comes up regarding coverage of sex crimes, from whether to name the victim to how to handle the right of the accused to be presumed innocent. To be covered by the media in association with a sex crime, whether the victim or accused, is to be opened up to merciless exposure of one's past, one's personality, particularly one's sex life.

The press' eagerness to examine the life of the accused is understandable, if sometimes objectionable. The press takes on the role of the detective in any crime, looking into the reasons for why that crime might have happened. And in my view, that role is often proper.

The only problem with the press becoming detective in this manner is that in practice the result tends to suggest that the accused is assumed guilty until proven innocent. Indeed, sometimes even after proven innocent. This is troubling enough. But, in sex crimes, the same practice of delving into the subject's private life also applies to victims, and this is where I think the press has gone tragically wrong.

The accepted practice of the moment is for the press to look into the life and personality of any woman who is the victim of a notorious sex crime. Thus, we have the last hours of the 1986 preppy murder victim, Jennifer Levin, covered minute by minute by the New York *Daily News*, under the classic victim-blaming headline, "How Jennifer Courted Death."

The Central Park jogger's parents were stalked by New York *Post* reporters. Patricia Bowman was unflatteringly profiled by the *New York Times* before the accused assailant, William Kennedy Smith, was even indicted. The sex life and motivation of Desiree Washington, Mike Tyson's victim, were scrutinized and criticized.

All of these people were subject, against their will, to exposures of their life style, their sexual tastes, and other people's opinion of them.

> *"Why do the media assume a sex crime victim's life or personality is relevant to the crime?"*
> —Helen Benedict

Why do the media assume a sex crime victim's life or personality is relevant to the crime? They don't look into the past of a liquor store owner whose shop is robbed—unless they suspect drug connections or something. They don't analyze the personality of a woman who was mugged on her way home from work. They don't examine the love life of a man whose apartment has been burgled. But as soon as sex comes into the equation, whether as rape, incest, molestation, murder, or harassment, the victim is instantly suspect. . . . "Kennedy Rape Gal Exposed"—a revealing headline. Who is the villain in that headline?

Why does the press distrust the victims of sex crimes so?

The answer is simple. Because the press is still entrenched in two myths: that women provoke sexual attacks, and that women who say they've been raped are usually lying. The reason the press is still entrenched in these myths, as I argue in my book, is because myths and stereotypes, or mental clichés as I call them, offer narratives that are quick and easy and require no thought. A lazy, but seductive way to report.

As a result of my research for *Virgin or Vamp*, I've come to question why victims are covered at all. Why is the victim treated in the same way as the accused? The victim committed no crime. It is not a crime to walk into one's home, go jogging in a park, go for a walk with a man on a beach, go on a date, pick up someone in a bar, go dancing, or flirt. It is not even a crime to go to bed with someone other people might consider dangerous. Some of these behaviors may seem unwise or dangerous, but they are not criminal.

Yet, the digging into the victim's past and personality, which is done routinely by the media, assumes that her past will reveal something about the crime—just as it might for the accused. Every profile of a victim, every account of what the victim does or has done, in the context of breaking crime, is therefore by implication an assumption that the victim had a role in causing the crime. In short, the very act of profiling the victim treats her as if she is guilty until proven innocent.

Am I seriously suggesting that crime reporting should be revised to the extent of actually never including profiles of the victim? I am. The press can educate the public about the truth of sexual assault by exploring the circumstances of the crime and the strength or weakness of the case against the accused, by explaining what rape is and why it happens, and by giving statistics that show that sexual assault can happen to anyone. To accomplish this, the press doesn't need to delve into the private life of the victim.

Helen Benedict's Suggestions for Coverage of Sex Crimes

1. All reporters assigned to a crime beat should educate themselves about rape. Newspapers should institute a policy requiring such training of their crime and trial reporters so the crime is no longer covered in the appalling ignorance in which it is now covered.

2. If a crime becomes a big news event, the paper should assign a reporter to stay outside the daily hurly-burly of the case, maybe someone like an ombudsman. He or she should research issues and write an analysis of the case from a distant perspective. This outside observer would try to redress the imbalances committed by the reporters enmeshed in the daily report of the news.

3. My most simple and radical recommendation is to stop publishing profiles of the victims as part of crime stories altogether. Instead—and this is where I throw out my challenge to you—concentrate on the much more difficult and much more valuable question of why rape, incest, sexual assault, or harassment happen at all.

The real reasons the press includes profiles of victims in its sex crime coverage are hardly educational. The most common, although unconscious one, is to lay the blame at her door. The other reason is simply a prurient one. The reader has been forced to imagine a victim taking part in degrading acts of sex, ". . . so let's tell them even more about her." This last reason is nothing more than catering to sexual voyeurism, which is not, in my view, an appropriate or desirable role for the respectable press.

If a person has propelled him or herself to public attention through intentional acts, relevant press scrutiny is justified. But a crime victim has not chosen to be a newsmaker. Going to the police to report a victimization should not be equated with seeking attention from the public at large.

The victim of a sex crime has been forced against her will to become part of a case. That does not justify invading her private life.

Patricia Bowman

Victims' Rights Advocate, Jupiter, FL
(Central figure in the William Kennedy Smith rape trial)

Less than 12 hours (after I reported the rape), my doorbell was ringing and the media were there. It wasn't one member, and it wasn't 20 members. There were somewhere near 100 members of the media outside my home within 24 hours of the crime. There were satellite trucks—you name it, they were there.

> *"I don't want my tombstone to say, 'Rape Victim.'"*
> —*Patricia Bowman*

Here is this confused, traumatized mind and body trying to grasp what the heck these people are doing here and one of the most important aspects of my perception at that time was I had no idea why a person rapes. I did not know. I did not know if that meant he would come back and kill me. I did not know if he knew where I lived. . . . I knew that if the media had found me, therefore, the man who had attacked me could then also find me.

At what time should the media approach a crime victim? The three most stressful times for a crime victim are immediately after the assault, during the trial, and the anniversary reactions. Now, for a hot story, I think you all say, when do you send reporters out? Immediately after the assault, during the trial, and during the anniversary reaction. All that does is increase any anxiety.

As a human being, I feel I have the right to recover when I want to recover, how I want to recover, and the amount of time it takes me to recover. My recovery shouldn't be intimidated or delayed by the media.

On Objections to Cameras in the Courtroom

Certainly. Because it is another thing that a victim has to deal with when she enters the courtroom. Most important for her is that it is conceivably the first time that the victim will have to see her assailant after the assault was committed, which is a very intimidating factor. But then to realize that all of this is going to be captured in a permanent record is extremely intimidating.

On Her Reaction to the *New York Times* Story Revealing Her Name

Rape takes away the ability to control and it takes away some of your belief system. That is that you have a safe body, and a right to your body—so that is gone. Then, you deal with the police, who you grow up believing are going to help you and assist you—and that one is gone, too. Your belief that the criminal justice system is there to serve all of the public—well, that one is gone.

Then, I saw another institution, another belief system, and that is that the old gray lady is the most respected form of journalism that you all have and that I have. I guess the best way for me to finish that one up is that all the news that is fit to print is not necessarily fit to read.

On Being a Public Figure Who Deserves Public Scrutiny

I still find it really funny that I am a public figure. I never ran for office. I never did anything terribly wrong. I never reached out for stardom or anything that in a naive mind says "public figure." But instantaneously [I am a public figure]—not only a national one, but internationally. People know my name, and know that I am a rape victim.

I do not want my tombstone to say, "Rape Victim." And I feel that is what will be in the minds of the public because of this case. I feel that is another assault against me, and that I have to work to change that image. If I do not, that is what somebody is going to remember me by.

Elinor Brecher

**Fashion Editor, *Miami Herald*
and Author of a controversial feature story, "The Mini-Skirt Rape Case,"
exposing a prostitute assaulted by a customer.**

[The Patricia Bowman case] was yet another instance in which an alleged victim's private life was being dissected in public, her lifestyle, habits, and associations picked at and prodded in lurid detail, perhaps not for the express purpose of putting her on trial but certainly with that result.

I found it sickening and infuriating, especially since some news organizations chose to use Bowman's name, essentially destroying whatever small chance she may still have had of protecting herself and her young child.

Inevitably, this generated an orgy of media navel-gazing on the issue of privacy in sex-abuse cases. On one side are those who think the press can help destigmatize rape by shining its cleansing light upon the victim. On the other are those who believe that women who have been sexually abused can only be harmed by unwanted attention and will be driven, by fear, out of the criminal justice system.

I believe that forcing publication of rape victims' names is no more justifiable than outing gay people or revealing that someone has AIDS, unless there is some overwhelmingly significant reason.

Let me assure you, anyone who thinks that publishing a rape victim's name in the newspaper AGAINST HER WILL is doing her a favor has never known a rape victim, and needless to say, has never been raped.

I have always found it interesting that some of the same people who vocally support women's choice on other issues of personal control, such as reproductive rights, think it is a dandy idea to force women, many of whom might be just one obscene phone call away from insanity or suicide, into the role of unwilling martyr to social change.

On the "Mini-Skirt Rape Case"

A 22-year-old woman told police she'd been kidnapped and raped by a drifter who accosted her outside an all-night Denny's, driven off in her own car at knifepoint, and terrorized for 5 hours until the man wrecked the car and Good Samaritans rescued her. She had been wearing [a white mesh mini-] skirt, a tank top, and high heels. She was not wearing underwear.

[Due to understaffing, The *Miami Herald*] missed key testimony that clearly demonstrated the degree to which the woman lied about herself and the incident, lied so blatantly that any jury with the collective IQ of a parking meter would have met reasonable-doubt standard and reached the same conclusion.

The drifter was acquitted. The same journalists once again failed to look past the obvious, which in the case was the jury foreman's remark, "She was asking for it, the way she was dressed." [Journalists] never bothered to ask for elaboration, such as, "Just exactly what

> "Let me assure you, anyone who thinks that publishing a rape victim's name in the newspaper AGAINST HER WILL is doing her a favor, has never known a rape victim, and needless to say, has never been raped."
> —*Elinor Brecher*

do you mean by 'it'—What else played into the verdict?"

National attention ensued as women's advocacy groups and media outlets latched onto the words of the foreman and the degree to which the clothing that the woman was wearing played into the verdict.

National experts who knew absolutely nothing about the case and had heard not a syllable of testimony pontificated about how it was a textbook example of our culture's Neanderthal treatment of sex-crime victims.

No one ever bothered to check that virtually everything she said about herself—or deliberately declined to say—was for the single purpose of concealing that she was a hooker. The "rape," as it turned out, was a "john deal" gone south.

The victim and her attorney lunged at every chance to parlay the situation into cash. She swept the talk shows and tabloids, which paid handsomely for her tale—under pseudonyms and wigs, repeating, unchallenged, the most preposterous fictions.

After watching [the alleged rape victim] at close range from the *Oprah Winfrey* studio audience, I became convinced that [the *Herald*] had fallen into one manipulative trap after another, and thus had seriously blown the story. I was hired to write a story about the alleged rape and Blandina Chiapponi's actions after it for a publication called *Tropic*. The first editorial decision we made was to use her name, for two reasons: There had been an acquittal. Therefore, in the eyes of the law, there had been no crime—no crime, no victim. Second, Blandina Chiapponi, the alleged victim, was aggressively marketing herself in the mass media. By her own choice and design, she had become a public figure.

For a few utterly surreal weeks, I submerged myself in Blandina's world, a world bounded by massage parlors, discos, and private-apartment orgies, peopled by transsexual whores, drug dealers, and petty criminals, fueled by cocaine. During the day, I hunkered down over court records. By night, I tailed her. There were times we were so close she could have plucked lint off my sweater, but she never knew who I was.

An invasion of privacy? Some people thought so, including some of my colleagues. I frequently ran up against resistance from other women at the paper, some of whom thought that unmasking Blandina amounted to condoning sexual abuse based on her line of work, clearly an antifeminist perspective. But, knowing how difficult it is in general for women in rape cases, I felt just the opposite. The last thing that women with authentic claims of sexual violence need is anyone perpetuating the pernicious view that women often yell rape to camouflage consent.

Helen Benedict

Responding to Elinor Brecher

The idea that an acquittal means that there was no crime and therefore no victim is simply untrue. And anyone who knows anything about rape trials and how they work—and any lawyer—will tell you this.

The rules of evidence in rape cases are extremely hard to meet. The rule of reasonable doubt means that the rules of evidence have to be pretty strong. There are almost no witnesses.

There are two kinds of rape: One is where they know there was a rape, but they are not sure if they have the right man. And the other is where they know who the man was but they are not sure whether it was consensual or not. Very often the right man was not caught, or the proof was not strong enough. That does not mean the woman was not a victim. You simply cannot make that assumption.

I guess what bothers me the most about that piece was Elinor's idea that you can somehow vindicate real victims by going after the assumed liars. I would say that that's self-defeating, because it only boosts the myth that the vamps, or really any woman with a sexual past, cannot be raped.

Also, just because a woman is a prostitute does not mean she cannot be raped. Just because a man is a john does not mean that he could not rape her. It is the same mistake that we see in trial after trial.

Tom French

Special Assignments Reporter, *St. Petersburg Times*
Recent works have entailed a year or more of intensive, "full-immersion" reporting

It is my experience, generally speaking, that the women I interview at length—where I spend months or a year with someone talking to them off and on—that the women I talk to and those I connect with in an intense way are generally much more sensitive to their own feelings and have a much keener understanding of how they feel about things and what has happened in their lives than are the men I generally interview.

I think that they are much more sensitive to what I write about because I think that there are all sorts of really destructive stereotypes and labels and things that women deal with all the time and men never have to.

On His Treatment of Subjects and Sources

I really think that the longer I do this, there is one sort of rule and that is I try to tell [sources and subjects] everything that I can about what is going to happen. We were talking about the loss of control that happens to rape victims and other victims, and I have written a lot about that as well. I think there is a general loss of control when

> *"Even when you are written about in a positive story, a story that describes you in glowing terms, it is a disorienting and difficult thing to go through."*
> —Tom French

you are written about that is a frightening thing. Even when you are written about in a positive story, a story that describes you in glowing terms, it is a disorienting and difficult thing to go through.

What I say to people up front, all the time now, when I do a detail story is: This is what I plan to do. This is tentatively how I plan to do it. It can change, but this is what I am thinking now. This is when I think it might run. This is where I think it might run. I also say that I cannot make any guarantee to you that you are going to like any of it, that you are going to like all of it or any of it; I hope you will. But I try to be up front about that. It does not preclude there being a misunderstanding at the end, but I think it helps.

The Private I, You, They

By J. T. Johnson
Sartor Associates

❏*Data pertaining to individuals and their life histories is no longer stored in physically accessible media. Instead, ink-on-paper data are rapidly being replaced with electronic bits and bytes literally scattered around the world, stored in various computers. Because most of these computers are linked to each other through the global telecommunications web, it is possible to assemble a digital persona of individuals without their ever knowing their electronic parallel personalities have been created, bartered, or sold by commercial interests. Or investigated by journalists. Such access to heretofore personal data raises new questions for the journalist and society about exactly what constitutes the individual and how privacy is to be defined in the digital age.*

Americans today are in a crucial period in a major revolution in the history of humanity. It is the second revolution in how we create, store, and exchange data, analyze it, and communicate the resulting information to others. During the first epoch of the history of information, everything that was known was stored in the minds of individuals and communicated by sound or action. Typically, individuals engaged in the communications process needed to be within sight or hearing of each other.

Then, sometime between 2,800 and 3,200 B.C.E. (Before the Common Era), writing was invented and the first revolution was imperceptibly underway. No longer was information shackled by human recollection or the boundaries of personal space and time. Data could be replicated and exchanged with exactness. Information could be challenged with other records. Texts and the ideas they implied and carried could be examined, debated, reinterpreted. Records of a business or government were created, challenged, and corrected. Rolls of a group of believers in a deity were kept and periodically known to the individuals in question. A person's access to his or her data was at least conceivable; corrections—or suppression of certain aspects—possible.

But a hundred years ago, data about individuals began to be stored mechanically and in a language that could not be read without the aid of a unique code book and mechanical devices.

Herman Holerith's cards—the initial IBM cards—were first used to compile the census of 1890. Those cards, with holes or no holes in a coded pattern, were the direct forerunner of today's digital computers. Such storage systems, holding not much more information than traditional parish records, were limited in content, accessible only by a few individuals, and confined to a few physical locations.

The early mechanical computers were not usually perceived as a threat to individuals. Those devices were seen in their day as further evidence of America's technological marvels. They were tantalizing suggestions of the promise of the 20th century. But that was the dream. And today there is a pragmatic issue in all this. What I see happening today is a shift from the print epoch, where data leading to information are stored in print form, to the digital epoch, where data are stored in strings of zeros and ones.

In this digital era, traditional literacy per se will be worthless in drawing on that data to generate information. By information, I mean that data which, upon analysis, we can use to help make a decision on anything.

The generalized, sweeping point I wish to make is that the digital revolution is not coming: It's here! And in a variety of forms.

Here's what's happening, even as we sit.

First, extremely large and highly varied quantities of data pertaining to individuals are being collected and stored electronically. But not all the data about one person are stored in a single computer. Keep that image in mind. Not all the data or information about you are in a single place.

Second, one way to think about that stored data is by asking: "How easy or difficult is it for anyone—either the subject or a third party—to get at those data?" Allow me to introduce some sophisticated jargon here, a taxonomy of data type. We'll call it "easy-access stuff," "moderate-access stuff," and "difficult access stuff."

Easy-access stuff includes things like name, age, date of birth, height, weight, social security number, and so forth. Moderate-access stuff includes credit cards you hold and your credit standing, court convictions, divorce records, property transfers. Difficult-access stuff includes things like a list of what you buy at the grocery, drug, or liquor store, health records, videotape rentals, cable programming watched, and what products, services, or publications you order by mail. The second factor about the digital epoch is that the data are stored in multiple (sometimes redundant), physically dispersed locations. The third point is that data are accessible over a telecommunication/computer matrix.

I have been studying, and using, this information matrix—"Surfing the info net" as hip Californians say—for nearly 10 years now. And for the past 4 or 5 years, I have been trying to find some social/cultural model to explain what was going on, something to help me to understand the significance and implications of the digital matrix. What does the existence of the matrix really mean to citizens? To journalists? Somehow, I really do not remember exactly how, puzzling over these questions has led me to the larger issue of privacy. And the study of privacy, I have discovered, is at once a daunting task and at the same time the most intriguing topic I have encountered. It is intriguing because privacy is a term we use all the time, and yet its definitions are as mushy as unbaked bread. Still, the concept is part of our profession's working assumptions. We believe that first, there is this thing called privacy and as reporters we have limits as to how far we can go in "invading" someone's privacy. Those limits are (a) officially imposed by legal decision, which really have a very short tradition, at least in American law; (b) legal decisions that have changed and will change; and (c) the legal definition of the boundaries of privacy as the culturally acceptable and appropriately sanctioned limits of the concept accepted by most reporters. But then I was struck with the more confounding question: Exactly what is privacy? Other than what the lawyers and judges and interpretation of cases say, are there different types and degrees of privacy? I did not know then. I do not know now. And I have not found anyone else who does, either. Are there universals—archetypes—of privacy that are shared by individuals and cultures? And perhaps the most perplexing question of all, one that coyly offers promise of resolution but simultaneously drapes a veil of incomprehension: When we speak of "loss of privacy," what exactly have we lost? Is it something like the camera stealing part of the soul?

Those questions have not yet been answered, but I came to realize a couple of things. First, the concept of privacy is rooted in the concept of the individual. Diabolical, tasseled-loafered lawyers from corporations and agencies might claim that a corporation has a right to privacy, but they do so without much success. If a group of corporations—or Ivy League schools—get together and try to protect their mutual privacy, they will be talking to someone from the FTC or the Anti-Trust division who just might think there's a whiff of monopolistic activity in the air. At least we hope so.

No, privacy—whatever that is—is something generally acknowledged to be a right of the individual. But this is where the digital matrix kicks in.

What is the individual in digital form? Here we can get into some heavy-duty philosophy and theology. Is the individual this body and this blood? Or is it something less tangible, something like the soul? What if we think of the individual as a walking collection of data, of demographic variables personified? That's exactly what we embody to a gang of businesses and bureaucrats around the world.

Here's how it works: Remember I suggested earlier that you not pay too much attention to the idea that there is information about you sitting in a single computer. Here's why: Imagine that among the literally thousands of data bases there are four: The Department of Motor Vehicles (DMV), your local water and sewer commission, a company called Neodata, and the Medical Information Bureau.

Each of these has some information about you, but no one of these knows everything about you—your variables personified. Understand, too, that it matters not a whit where these data bases are. In the old days of print, the physical location of the data was everything. If a reporter wanted to get someone's military record, he or she would at least have to call Washington and hope to find a friendly clerk who would dig it out.

Even today, when the political appointees in the State Department wanted to track down Bill Clinton's passport records, they had to literally go to the warehouse and paw through boxes. Rather quaint, don't you think? When we're dealing with digital data bases, however, space and time are of little or no consequence. Electrical signals move at the speed of light. So when someone dials into the DMV records here in Florida, it's a lot faster than going to Tallahassee or making the rounds of each county. And you don't have to worry about office hours. Note, too, that to be in one data base, theoretically, is to be in all because, for very good reasons, most are on the telecommunications matrix. They have to communicate with each other. Here, then, we can see how someone, benign or otherwise, can start to "build" an individual—not a person who represents variables personified, but rather a digital persona.

First, a few pieces of information are teased out of one data base. These data are information itself, but they also contribute to a larger composite character, a mosaic. And when the searcher concludes there is no more pertinent information in the data base, he or she moves on to the next, gathering a string of variables, gradually assembling an ever larger parallel personality.

One of the interesting questions, I think, is: At what point does this parallel personality become viable? That is, at what point is it a "living thing"?

I think the answer is that whenever a collection of information reaches the point where it has value in the marketplace it reaches viability, that is, when someone will pay hard cash or barter for that specific parallel personality. This is not the future, of course. This is happening to each of us right now. There are multiple, parallel personalities being created for each of us by companies like Neodata, which claims to have information on 85% of households in America. It claims to have up to 900 pieces of information on each of those families. Why? Because Neodata and its peers are selling your parallel personalities—according to some estimates, 190 times a year.

What does all this have to do with privacy? First, if privacy is a concept tied to the individual, as I suggested earlier, then these parallel personalities can only exist so long as we are alive—as consumers of products or government services or able to vote. I've yet to hear of demand for a mailing list of dead folks.

Second, the one common thread I've discovered in reviewing the literature for definitions of privacy is the right of the individual to control—to control information about him- or herself. The lawyers tend to think of privacy as a matter of property, I believe, whereas the social scientists think of it as control of information. Therefore, what has happened to control over that information once it's in the digital matrix? Our parallel personalities are being bought and sold daily, and we don't have a damn thing to say about it. And that's today's action. What about tomorrow's?

How many of you have heard of "knowbots"? Imagine how a virus—perhaps a worm would be a better example—can move through the telecommunications matrix, from one computer to the next. Imagine, then, a good virus, or worm, an agent which you program with some instructions and say, "Fetch." Instructions for the Knowbot could be: "Jay Black, University of South Florida. Go see what you can find about Jay Black, Knowbot."

And off it goes, a small program wending its way through the matrix like a drift net, picking up anything and everything that satisfies, initially, the instructions "Jay Black. University. South Florida." And the Knowbot learns as it goes, gathering more information and learning that Jay Black is really—or at least there's a high probability—John Jay Black.

Make your blood boil, citizens? Sure. At first glance. But were the issue that simple. Were the guys in the black hats so easily identifiable? Reflect for a moment that many of the same variables being used by the direct mailing houses and the telephone boiler room is information used to plan the nation's health care system, build its schools, and apportion the number of representatives and tax dollars to each state. It's the same information used to project your retirement packages. And here, then, we come to the real dilemma for journalism and for the citizens.

If we assume that so much private, individual data are potentially available, how shall we define privacy? Does the capability of the digital matrix to create these parallel personalities have any impact on the Fourth Amendment, with its search and seizure provision? How can we, as citizens, determine what information shall always remain in the custody of the individual versus what personal, individual information is needed by our own government to provide for our common good? Specifically, what are the implications of this for journalism?

First, if we're going to both use and report on the implications of the digital revolution, or the information revolution, we need to learn for ourselves how the system works.

Second, we need to strive to get the debate on digital privacy in the public arena so that we can, first, enlighten the citizenry. If we don't educate our readers, I fear there will be some catalyst—something like the search for Bill Clinton's passport information—that's going to set off some draconian legislation. A Jesse Helms or Ross Perot, or a Bill Clinton, will ride that issue straight into office. And the pressure will be to close all data doors to public examination.

Consequently, citizens or reporters simply won't be able to find out how many drunken school bus drivers there are in their state.

Finally, editors can create an information beat. Get your smartest general assignment reporter and put him or her on the case. There will be stories on education, business, economics, and politics. And, perhaps, there will be stories on nothing less than the very essence of democracy itself. That is, the individual and his or her sense of privacy.

Some Paradoxes of Privacy

By Nora Paul
Poynter Institute for Media Studies

❑*The ease of access to public records information and the growth of records derived from commercial transactions have created paradoxes for the journalist. "The right to know" and "the right to privacy" are sometimes in conflict. This article outlines some of these paradoxes and raises some issues for the practice of journalism created by these paradoxes.*

There's a saying my mother always used when one of us kids paid back someone who was being mean. Maybe you've heard it: "Two wrongs don't make a right." Well, for the purposes of this conference, I think we could flip it around a bit to "Two rights just might make a wrong." In this case, the rights I'm referring to are the right to privacy and the public's right to know.

One issue being played out in newsrooms is whether the fact that information has been found necessarily means it must be made public: the right to protect a private citizen from public disclosure of facts about their lives versus the public's right to access to information. It comes down basically to, "I've got this information, should I use it in my story?"

One of the main reasons that information access is such a big concern these days is that information about individuals, thanks to computers, is more abundant and more cheaply and easily accessed than ever before.

In the old days of investigative reporting, following the paper trail on someone was time consuming, requiring trips to the courthouse and dealing with surly clerks and sorting through files and reports looking for the instances when your subject was mentioned. The only people you took that kind of time and effort to track were major offenders or people whose actions affected the public in some way: politicians, mafiosos, slum lords. And the stories that would use this kind of information were major pieces, worked on for weeks or months. But now, the paper trail has gone electronic, and reporters have at their fingertips, 24 hours a day, in the comfort and chaos of their own newsrooms, the means to access personal information on private citizens. Background checks are routine in most major newsrooms, mostly because they are easy to do.

Those who are attempting to deal with privacy concerns by legislating closed access to government records are shutting the barn door behind the cows. The biggest consumer of government records, the files that Big Brother is keeping on you, is big business.

Although most of this information now available via computer has always been gathered in some form, the computer access has given rise to some issues that never arose when the information was on paper filed away in a cabinet.

Some of those issues are:

1. We could do it, but it would be wrong: Awareness that information is there and available makes for tough calls. At the *Miami Herald,* we got access to a data-base service that provided access to credit records on individuals. We would access only the part of the record that had the header information: current and previous addresses, spouse's name, social security number, current and previous employment. However, some of the reporters knew that behind that front screen, there was the full credit information. We would not search it, because it was illegal to, not so much because it was unethical to.

2. The possibility of making connections that would have been difficult if not impossible and certainly time consuming before. Suddenly the abstract becomes real. We spent a lot of time trying to track down Ron Reagan, Jr. We tracked down neighbors and public records to locate him because we wanted to find out if he had AIDS as it had been rumored. I finally said, "Why are we doing this? Leave him alone," but the argument that his father was someone considered responsible for ignoring the AIDS problem and, therefore, his son having AIDS made it a news story, made sense.

3. Things that were intended to be private or not disclosed, such as memberships in private clubs, now can be discovered and disclosed. If the club does not want to give out membership information because its members don't want it known, would it be unethical to get and publish a membership list? But tap into *Who's Who* in data-base form and you can search for people belonging to a particular club. There are many ways to track down people without their realizing it. If you are looking for jurors in a case, you can look in the parking lot, get license tags, and run a search. If you can do it, is it wrong? Are these methods a way to get around bureaucracy, and have the ways that were used in the past to prevent disclosure not caught up to the information age?

4. The press is having to be duplicitous, and it occasionally throws the privacy people a bone. For instance, in Florida, privacy supporters want to start blocking the address information on driver's license records. I keep saying, fine, don't raise a stink, throw them that bone, maybe it will make them forget about the fact that a social security number is on the record, too. And if you have that, you've got all you need to get the rest. There are lots of ways to get addresses.

Here's a short list of paradoxes of the press and privacy. Consider that:

1. Journalists fight for "government in the sunshine" and open records

but fight anyone who wants to know how reporters do business and protect their records.

2. They want to reveal secrets about others but don't want others to know their secrets, their confidential sources.

3. They may be using public records and pulling up private data about people, but if others do the same thing, they are all over them.

4. They write condemning stories of others who do the very things they do (people pulling together data bases of prescription sales by individual got bad press), but media organizations are doing it themselves, as with data-base marketing of subscribers and what they buy.

5. Journalists are the worst about giving out information about themselves. Many journalists refuse to give interviews, but a public figure who refuses to grant an interview usually is cast in a very negative light.

6. Within a news organization there are information conflicts between newsroom and business sides. It is almost impossible to get information from the subscribers' data base.

7. Newspapers clamor about public records access, yet they are the most proprietary about sharing their own data when they've made it. One computer-assisted reporting editor who spent a lot of time putting a campaign finance data base together, when asked if he was making copies available, said aghast, "No, that's my data," even though the "public good" argument should have been in effect.

8. Newspapers write about errors in credit reports or misinformation in public records, but are reluctant to fully disclose their own errors in accuracy or to correct mistakes in the record of their reporting about people.

9. Reporters look forward to being able to use caller-ID to see who is calling them but have embraced the caller-ID blocking technology so they can screen others from seeing that they are calling. (They are using "Private Lines," a 900 number that scrambles calls.)

10. Sometimes by trying to "help" victims by illustrating their life or background, reporters are, in fact, hurting them by invading their privacy.

The Right Versus the Need to Publish

By Robert Ellis Smith
Publisher of *Privacy Journal*

Journalists do two things that are kind of contradictory about privacy. First, they disparage it . . . and at the same time . . . they overstate what privacy actually means. They really view it as a bugaboo that covers virtually everything that will prevent them from doing any of the credible stories that they want to do. It is neither.

Privacy protects only sensitive personal information. All of the court cases say that. Not everything about an individual is entitled to privacy protection, and it, of course, depends on the context. One's name and address may be innocuous in some context, but in another context, may well raise a privacy issue.

It is no longer paranoid to protect your address. You want that to be confidential. I don't think that a lot of journalists have caught up with the fact that where you live can make you extremely vulnerable to others. There can be no complaint of an invasion of privacy if there is consent of the news subjects. It is important to realize, though, that the law will recognize that you can withdraw consent after you have once given it. After you figure out the direction that the story is going, you can certainly withhold consent—and that is as if you had never given it up in the first place.

The passage of time can create a privacy right that did not exist when the information was first uncovered. This is where newspapers get in the most trouble with lawsuits. The right to privacy diminishes virtually to zero in death. It is possible in a very select number of cases that information about a dead person reflects on those who are still living and may invade their privacy. The right to privacy is uniquely a personal right. Organizations do not possess any privacy rights. That is thrown out to newspaper people and a lot of people fall for it. "I'm not going to tell you about the air pollution that we have in our company because of privacy." There is no such right. Companies have certain interests in trade secrets that are recognized, but that is not a privacy right, which is individual. We have had ample evidence that intrusion upon one's solitude causes real pain and the pain is for a long period, often for a lifetime, and it can threaten one's personal security. We are in a time where we should think about the personal security of news subjects, as well as their pain and suffering which formerly was the extent of the concern.

There is an absolute right to publish. But in my mind, there is no right to know. I do not think any court has really established that there is a constitutional right to know. There is an absolute right to publish, but there is no immunity from later consequences from something that is published. There is an absolute right to publish, there is not always an absolute need to publish.

Privacy freaks are thought to be wanting to impose some sort of censorship in the press. In fact that is not true. We are not talking about government and saying you cannot publish things. We are talking about self-restraint. Standards that will not only restrain certain coverage, but also provide more leeway in what is covered. There is a lot more leeway in the privacy area than I think a lot of working journalists realize.

Privacy Guidelines

- Just because information is published in one place does not make it public property everywhere.
- The more innocent the newsworthy behavior, the higher the entitlement to privacy protection. Having an illness is not evidence of wrongdoing, though a lot of stories lead you to believe otherwise. So the claim to privacy protection should be higher in the case of say, sexual misconduct. By the same token, if the claim to privacy is high and the newsworthiness marginal, then I think the privacy claim has to prevail.
- We are not all open targets for press coverage. Reporters and editors should give special consideration to publicity impact on children of people in the news. We, as journalists, have to be much more sensitive to that. Even if the children are not the subject of the story, what is the impact on the children?
- When personal privacy is involved, reporters and editors should take extra time and care in delaying a story, if necessary, to reexamine its accuracy, its newsworthiness, and its negative impact on the individuals involved. The *New York Times* came up with this. It is a post-Patricia Bowman rule. That is now their rule. If they write a story that involves personal information about people, they will now take that extra time to give it an extra look.
- Reporters should instinctively assume that any government document concerning an individual is inaccurate or misleading. I'm not speaking legally now, but [describing] moral protection for journalists. I'm really shocked that after all we know about how inefficient government is, we still think that if it is in a government document, that it has the presumption of truth. I would like to reverse that and say that it is the presumption of error.
- The ultimate question for a reporter is: Would I deserve to live with the consequences if the information was published about me? I point out the rule that I use, which is "deserve," not "like." We all run stories that people don't like, and they have to live with it for the rest of their lives even if they don't like it. My point was "deserve." Do they deserve to live with the consequences of that story? It might well relate back to the rule about weighing the conduct versus the invasion of privacy. Those whose conduct certainly raises questions of ethics and criminality deserve to live with the consequences of having that published.

— Robert E. Smith

Rephrasing Some Rules First Articulated to Robert Smith by Congressman Barney Frank

In addition to sensitivity training that you might well be prompted to have with regard to victims, I would hope too that you would invite into your newsroom for your staffs a politician who can reflect on the impact of publicity and news gathering on his or her family and on his or her work. I think you might get a grasp of how the current mania in the news business is really depriving these people of their personhood and making them lesser public servants.

For public officials, there is a right to privacy, but not a right to hypocrisy. The press should be hard on politicians who vote one way and conduct their lives in a different way. The people who make the rules should be subject to them. There are private activities, such as alcohol or excessive sexual activities that impair one's abilities, and these should be exposed.

Public officials have a right to privacy, although one more diminished than the average citizen. The notion that you have no right to privacy because you are a public figure is nonsense, and I don't think most journalists realize that. I think they think that it is open season on anybody who is "crazy enough to run for public office." I think that is particularly unfortunate.

Activities that reflect negatively on one's character should be reported. Does private activity show a rotten personality? Abuse of a spouse is an example of private activity that should be reported publicly.

It is a fact of life that if the press likes [a politician] and the public likes [him or her], you get more of a free ride than otherwise. Perhaps a corollary of that rule is that if you have got a strong reservoir of public good will and political ability, you will survive a lot of these attacks.

Private activity that reveals a pattern of behavior is fair game. That rule will be defended in the coverage of Gary Hart.

One that disturbs me is that different rules apply to presidential candidates, and no one knows what they are.

Privacy is a shield, not a sword, and this is important. The press often has to protect politicians who use their positions to enhance their private activities but then yell "privacy!" By the same token, just because sex is involved does not immunize improper conduct.

The press should not keep quiet if it discovers a sexual partner of a famous person has undue influence or has been involved in improper conduct.

Certain private information like a politician's religious views ought not be reported. I am not sure that certain intimate information, including spiritual information, and how one exercises religion, whether one votes or not, how one votes, information in therapy, all of those things may well become relevant at some point, though I hope that we realize that those are the exceptions, not the rules.

Arthur Ashe said, "There were things in my life I wanted still to do that I can't do now." That is what he said about the disclosure. Not because of his health, but because of the publicity.

It is a matter of control. I do not think that journalists are sensitive to the fact that publicity is a one-way street. It does hamstring people's lives. It prevents them from doing the things that they want to do.

Why I Think Privacy Is Important to the Individual

It is important on the most personal intense level to people's lives and their autonomy. It is important in other ways as well as to the individual. Privacy provides safe haven for developing one's personality. We know that everything that we do that is public is really accountable, and we have to have safe havens in our lives to make mistakes, to do things that are crazy, do things that are embarrassing, to have false starts, to expand.

Why Privacy Is Important to the Society

I see the damage that irresponsible invasion of privacy by the press does to our society. I really think that it is cheapening our culture. It teases us. It does not teach us anything, it teases us.

It demeans people of accomplishment in public life—politicians, performers, athletes. It demeans their accomplishments. I think it distracts them. Journalists cannot quite get it through their heads that some people have to make a living on a stage and in the movies and even expose their bodies, and that still does not mean they do not have a zone of privacy.

> A Definition of Privacy:
> *Privacy is the claim of an individual to control when and how information will be disclosed.*

A lack of privacy deters a lot of talented people from entering these realms. We are losing a lot of talented people. We are percolating to the top of our political system only those who can survive this hazing and this ordeal—and I think this is particularly unfortunate.

We are not only deterring good people from public service, we apparently keep good people from reporting crimes, a basic civic responsibility.

A lot of this [news] coverage is so teasing. Essentially, it lets us live vicariously through the lives of someone else. That is what I resent the most about it. I think it allows us to continue in denial in our lives. We deny the reality of our own lives because we live vicariously through celebrities . . . not only live the glamour of Hollywood lives, but to also live the grief of other people's lives and I think it is sick.

Journal of Mass Media Ethics
Vol. 9, No. 4, pp. 235–242

Using Data Bases to Serve Justice and Maintain the Public's Trust

By Karon Reinboth Speckman
Stephens College

❏*Reporters' use of government data bases can create problems with serving justice and maintaining privacy. Although there are many advantages to the new reporting tool, problems can arise when the information is inaccurate or is misused for purposes other than originally intended. The ethical question of maintaining privacy while fulfilling the political function of the media is discussed. Suggested guidelines are given.*

Through the use of computers and government data bases, media are employing old-fashioned public records for new reporting coups. Examples of government data bases include voter registration records, criminal records, tax lists, and drivers' license records. Legally, news organizations may purchase government computer data bases. In so doing, they are simply accessing public records in a different form—old wine in new bottles, as it were.

Larger media organizations have been doing an admirable job of using state and federal data bases. However, as smaller and more financially strapped newsrooms begin to use data bases, they will need a framework of common sense principles to protect individuals' privacy. Also, as more city and county records are switched to computers, these data bases may not be as accurate as state or federal data bases, and specific precautions need to be taken. First, although media can use the new reporting tool to serve justice, they also must examine privacy issues to maintain a relationship of trust with the public. Second, media need to acknowledge the problems of accuracy and currency and consider proactive ethical solutions that transcend legal requirements.

This article examines several ethical issues of reporting with government data bases and the difficulty of fulfilling ethical obligations. Questions addressed are: What are the advantages of using the data bases? What are the trouble areas of data-base use? Can justice be served by data-base use? How is privacy defined? What are ethical choices? What can media organizations do?

Advantages of Using the Data Bases?

Employing government data bases in reporting can tip the balance of power by alerting the public to problems with government, thus fulfilling a crucial political function of the press (Hodges, 1986). Tipping the balance of power meshes with Rawls's (1985) theory of justice as fairness, which suggests that each person has an equal right to a fully adequate scheme of basic rights and liberties, with society as a system of fair social concern between free and equal persons. Often, ordinary citizens can only be assured of justice in society when media organizations can expose wrongdoing. *Data base journalism* aids citizens with stories that range from a Knight–Ridder investigation of high death rates resulting from open-heart surgeries to a *Providence Journal* article comparing lists of bus driver licenses with a computer tape of traffic violations (Stricharchuk, 1988). Other examples of government data-base use by media that served private citizens include analyzing loan data to describe and document racially discriminatory practices of lending institutions and examining a data base of state-financed home mortgages to show that loans benefited the wealthy rather than low and moderate income home buyers (Kleeman, 1989).

Using computers to analyze data bases can "only make a good reporter better," said Elliot Jaspin, former executive director of the Missouri Institute for Computer Assisted Reporting (personal communication, July 25, 1991). In addition to speeding up research by taking less time to sift through cumbersome documents, reporters can use statistical analysis to show relationships and trends such as documenting the relationship between campaign contributions and votes by state legislators (Garneau, 1985). Computer-assisted reporting not only can bring media organizations to a new level of activism in their reporting (Walker, 1990), but also can release reporters from the bonds of "event coverage" to ask questions about how institutions and government function (Burnham, as cited in Walker, 1990).

Using data bases may be the only way for media organizations of all sizes to survive in the reporting world, because so many paper records are being switched to computer. "If newspapers can't at least check on the government's analysis, then the press is in serious trouble," according to Jaspin (Bland, 1991, p. 12). Clearly, data-base reporting is an invaluable tool to assure that justice and fairness win over inequities and faceless bureaucracies.

Trouble Areas of Data-Base Use?

Brown (1990) identified five general areas where data-base control may give rise to ethical problems: gathering, storage, processing, retrieval, and use. Although these are usually problem areas for government and private corporations, media may face similar problems if only because media often copy the practices of other bureaucracies.

The first area—gathering—becomes a problem when data are gathered by government organizations for specific purposes and then are purchased by media, which can use the data for other purposes. For example, media organizations—generally those with marketing, advertising, or public relations arms—can match census data with postal addresses to develop mailing lists that are a goldmine of information about race, income, marital status, and so forth ("Ready to Zero In," 1991; Strnad, 1990). Nowak and Phelps (1991) asserted that this secondary use of personal information will not be known to consumer citizens. Media, being private economic enterprises, can be tempted to use newsgathering computer tapes for marketing purposes, particularly in difficult economic times.

Brown (1990) also suggested that the process of gathering or acquiring information often is indiscriminate, and information is then distorted to suit computer requirements. By separating the information from its original purpose, the information is stripped from its original context.

The second trouble area—long-term data storage—is troublesome because information that is inaccurate and out-of-date is kept for too long and the information often is unknown to and/or unchecked by the subject (Brown, 1990). For example, many crime data bases that may eventually be used by media contain errors. An Office of Technology Assessment (1988) report estimated that about 50% of arrest entries in the National Crime Information Center data base did not show disposition or resolution of the case, with errors in as much as 20% of arrest dispositional data. Laudon (1986) asserted that files of the FBI's national computerized criminal history system are inaccurate, incomplete, or ambiguous, making the data base especially damaging to minorities. The inaccuracy or nonconfidentiality of records can cost jobs or deny promotions: "Chances are if you do have the luck or perseverance to unearth these files, or to discover mistakes, you will very likely be helpless to do anything about them. Errors, once recorded, become accepted as truths" (Linowes, 1989, p. 11).

Brown's (1990) third and fourth trouble areas—processing and retrieving data—are problematic because there is an ease of compilation, abstraction, and access to the users but not to the subject. An example of computer information that was easily moved back and forth among agencies but was very difficult for the subject to correct was the Education Department's discovery through computer matching of a delinquent student loan (Davis, 1987). Unfortunately, two different people with the same name were confused in the computer program. The wrong person was identified as being in default. The Education Department threatened to report the default to the IRS and sent the inaccurate information to a private credit agency. A request for a car loan was rejected. Such inaccuracy problems justify journalists gaining special training so they can spot faulty data and draw correct conclusions from tapes.

The final trouble area, Brown (1990) said, is that data are often secretly used by the wrong people for the wrong reasons. For example, much information consumers provide to salespeople ends up being sold or rented to credit bureaus and marketing companies without consumer knowledge (Fost, 1990).

Can Justice Be Served by Data-Base Use?

Using data bases for citizens' good while protecting citizens from yet another peep show into their private lives should be of concern to news organizations. Media need to recognize the potential for conflict between serving justice and preserving privacy.

Christians (1986) challenged journalists to fulfill their duty of serving justice: "In a day when the powerless have few alternatives left, and virtually no recourse, should the press not serve as a voice, as a megaphone of sorts for those who cry out to be heard?" (p. 111).

Promoting justice is a challenge when privacy concerns are raised. If Rawls's (1971) justice as fairness concept is used, journalists would accept that they treat all parties in privacy cases as equal persons when deciding whether to use gathered information. Going behind the "veil of ignorance," all parties would exchange information for equitable decisions. As in all reporting, media have the responsibility to make sure information is available and accurate, especially information that government has collected. However, no one right, including privacy, automatically supersedes others. Media must realize that the rights to publish "curiosity" stories or corporation/government bashing stories based on data bases may lose out to privacy rights under the veil.

For instance, a media organization could use computer tapes to compare drivers' licenses with bus drivers' traffic violations, but it could also use the same data base to write a "cute" feature story describing the fattest person in the state. In both cases, rights of privacy compete with other rights, such as safety or the public's need to know. Obviously, safety and life questions prevail over privacy rights in the first instance, but privacy rights should prevail in the second, where idle if not prurient interest is the only competing value.

Hodges (1983) provides criteria for balancing justice and privacy: "It is just for a journalist to violate the privacy of an individual if and only if information about that individual is of overriding public importance and if the public need cannot be met by other means" (p. 12; also see Hodges's updated treatment of this topic in this issue of *JMME*). Hodges asserted that if information is important because it gives the public knowledge they need in order to function well, then a story is valuable. However, he said, "no story is important as an end in itself" (p. 13).

In Elliott's (1986) terms:

> If the readers/viewers need ... information to fulfill their societal expectations, as with information that would affect voting behavior, trust in local government, or understanding of the judicial process, then utilitarian precepts allow the harm of one in favor of the benefit of many. (p. 37)

Kultgen (1988) suggested a general test for balancing utility with justice: "If the injustice inflicted is great and the increment in utility is small, choose justice. If the utility is great and the injustice is small, choose utility" (p. 28).

Exclusive reliance on the virtue of justice could push journalists toward making general rules to promote the greatest general welfare, or rule utilitarianism. Because no all-encompassing general rules can be made in this arena, defining the elusive concept of privacy may offer a first step in serving justice.

How Is Privacy Defined?

Privacy is not an issue in stories that use government data bases to show trends. For example, using the drivers' license data base to show an unhealthy direction of higher weights in the state would not invade privacy because it would look at averages and not individual data. However, the potential for privacy invasion is present in stories using individual data. The concept of computer privacy is especially troublesome because of the ease and speed of finding out facts about people; even a quiet and unassuming person can be on file with the IRS (taxes), Veteran's Administration (veterans), State Department (passports), Social Security Administration, and Department of Education (student loans) (Linowes, 1989).

As our "private" information, thoughts, buying habits, records, and meetings come under surveillance and are stored in a computer's memory, we lose our individuality (Burnham, 1983). Burnham suggested this surveillance eventually poisons the soul of the nation by limiting personal options for citizens and increasing the power of those in a position to benefit from this activity.

Although privacy ideally is a right to which all are entitled because of their status as persons (Fried, 1984), Post (1989) suggested that enjoying the benefits of privacy may depend on economic class. If so, the abuse of privacy may be a class-based injustice, and an entire class of citizens lack the power to defend their rights against the abuse of computers.

Because privacy is not mentioned in lists of rights along with life, liberty, right not to be harmed, and property rights, Thomson (1984) called privacy a cluster right: "It is not a distinct cluster of rights, but itself intersects with the cluster of rights which the right over the person consists in and also with the cluster of rights which owning property consists in" (p. 281). Reporters therefore must balance privacy rights with other rights. If using a data base can serve justice by protecting life or liberty, then the right of privacy may have to be temporarily suspended. Although this relegates preserving privacy to a lower status than preserving justice, it does not ignore privacy. Instead, individual rights of privacy are balanced with other community rights in data bases that list individuals.

What Are the Ethical Choices?

Value conflicts occur as privacy and the responsibility of the press in serving justice are defined. Journalists and citizens value public records because those records help keep a democratic society open. Journalists value powerful investigative reporting tools because the tools aid in correcting the imbalance between the powerful and the disenfranchised. Journalists value the right to give that information to the public, fulfilling the "people's need to know." Journalists value accuracy because inaccuracy not only damages their profession but also endangers citizens' livelihoods. Americans value many of the services that modern society and bureaucracies give them, even at some cost to their individual privacy.

With all these conflicting values, how will ethical reporting decisions be made? Not using data-base reporting may be an abdication of media's responsibility to fulfill their political function. Because individual citizens often do not understand government information, media have the responsibility to use data-base reporting to help citizens by clarifying the volumes of information the government collects.

Likewise, it is not ethically responsible for media to avoid printing or broadcasting any information that has the potential to hurt individuals if that information will help readers/viewers fulfill their societal expectations. As stated previously, utilitarian precepts allow the harm of one in favor of the benefit of many (Elliott, 1986). However, Elliott ddid not believe that journalists fulfill their societal expectations without obligation: "The promise-based category obligates journalists to uphold the public trust in the journalistic craft and to give the audience what they have led readers or viewers to believe they will provide" (p. 39). If media acknowledge that the public distrusts computers in general, fulfilling the promise-based category may require taking special precautions as outlined in this article's concluding section.

What are media organizations' responsibilities regarding inaccuracies of data bases? Individuals often lack the power to correct inaccuracies through publicity. Private citizen rights may supersede those of large corporations or government agencies, who often are savvy to techniques of crisis communication. If inaccuracies are found, simply not using a data base may not go far enough. Media can broadcast or publish stories about the inaccuracies in data bases.

Brown (1990) suggested that recipients of personal information must not only have a legitimate use for it, but the purpose or use must also be connected in a positive way with the interests of the subject of that information. This separates legal rights from moral rights. Although media may have a legal right to public records, they must consider the rights of the subjects on the data bases. When justice is to be served and items from a data base can be tied to individuals, the data should be confirmed on the individual level (the bus drivers' story). However, when data bases are used to show trends (housing mortgage stories), every single item need not be checked if the data base is generally reliable. Spot checks would be appropriate, however.

What Can Media Organizations Do?

Data-base reporting will not, nor should it, disappear. However, news organizations of all sizes need to address the issues of privacy and inaccuracy. Media can begin to address those issues if they:

1. Acknowledge the use of a data base to the public when writing or broadcasting a story—just as a source is given. Simply saying that the story

was based on computer analysis may not be adequate to build trust. Special protection arrangements that have been made with the government while using the data base should be mentioned, along with the source of the data base and its age.

2. Treat a data base as a source to be thoroughly checked by taking the data base down to an individual case and then checking out that individual case against sources if possible. Triangulate the sources, just as reporters do with paper records. If a newsroom uses a specific bit of data from a data base instead of aggregate data, it should independently verify its accuracy.

3. Consider original intent when purchasing data bases. This does not mean that tapes cannot be kept and analyzed. But the tapes must be valued for their ability to change people's lives.

4. Articulate a policy not to sell or share government data bases. A survey of Fortune 500 companies revealed that 80% of them disclosed personal information to credit granters, 58% to landlords, and 25% to charitable organizations (Linowes, 1989). Private credit corporations such as TRW and Equifax profit by selling and sharing their information; news media should not do this at the risk of losing the public's trust. Computer tapes acquired by journalists should only be used for newsgathering, not marketing. For example, the *Providence Journal-Bulletin* does not let its circulation and advertising departments see or use the paper's acquired data-base records (Bender, 1987).

5. Budget money to purchase current data bases as others become out-of-date. Rawson (as cited in Bender, 1987) suggested that keeping tapes current requires a continuing commitment of time, money, and dedication to public service.

6. Continue to cooperate with the government on guidelines that protect privacy and those unable to protect themselves. In a 1984 study, the *Des Moines Register* wanted a printout from the state's computer system of all children listed as missing (Spencer, 1985). The *Register* worked with the courts to protect names of children who might have been stigmatized because they were juvenile offenders.

7. Place the raw data in a library or research facility to be examined by anyone. Provide the data analysis to experts to review and discuss and fill reasonable requests from readers for more data (Moore, as cited in Bender, 1987). Obviously, these procedures would have to be used with caution if individual data are contained on the data base.

8. Scrutinize data bases for dirty data and imperfect methodology (Stick, as cited in Bland, 1991). Moore (as cited in Bender, 1987) suggested that reporters must understand statistical measures and realize, for example, that a correlation is different from a cause.

9. Provide funds to train reporters and editors about computer-aided reporting techniques and how to correctly analyze data (Bland, 1991).

This is a very elementary list of common-sense principles when using government data bases.

New concerns and problems will arise as more news organizations begin to use data bases. However, the most difficult questions will remain:

"Why are we doing this story?" and "Whose interests are we serving? If news organizations can accept the ethical challenges of using data bases, the public's trust can be maintained while justice is served.

References

Bender, J. (1987, Fall). Computer records. *The IRE Journal*, pp. 12–16.

Bland, D. (1991, January/February). Computers can turn ordinary reporters into super sleuths. *The Bulletin of the American Society of Newspaper Editors*, pp. 11–15.

Brown, G. (1990). *The information game: Ethical issues in a microchip world.* Atlantic Highlands, NJ: Humanities Press International.

Burnham, D. (1983). *The rise of the computer state.* New York: Random House.

Christians, C. (1986). Reporting and the oppressed. In D. Elliott (Ed.), *Responsible journalism* (pp. 109–127). Beverly Hills, CA: Sage.

Davis, B. (1987, August 20). Abusive computers. *The Wall Street Journal*, p. 1.

Elliott, D. (1986). *Responsible journalism.* Beverly Hills, CA: Sage.

Fost, D. (1990, May). Privacy concerns threaten data base marketing. *American Demographics*, pp. 18–21.

Fried, C. (1984). Privacy, a moral analysis. In F. Schoeman (Ed.), *Philosophical dimensions of privacy: An anthology* (pp. 203–223). Cambridge, UK: Cambridge University Press.

Garneau, G. (1985, November 9). Computers as investigative tools. *Editor & Publisher*, p. 30.

Hodges, L. (1983). The journalist and privacy. *Social Responsibility: Journalism, Law, Medicine, 9*, 5–19.

Hodges, L. (1986). Defining press responsibility: A functional approach. In D. Elliott (Ed.), *Responsible journalism* (pp. 13–31). Beverly Hills, CA: Sage.

Hodges, L. (1994/this issue). The journalist and privacy. *Journal of Mass Media Ethics, 9*, 197–212.

Kleeman, R. (1989, September). Good hunting in data bases. *The Quill*, pp. 16–17.

Kultgen, J. (1988). *Ethics and professionalism.* Philadelphia: University of Pennsylvania Press.

Laudon, K. (1986). *Dossier society: Value choices in the design of national information systems.* New York: Columbia University Press.

Linowes, D. (1989). *Privacy in America: Is your private life in the public eye?* Urbana: University of Illinois Press.

Nowak, G., & Phelps, J. (1991, August). *Quenching the thirst for personal information: Advertising practices vs. consumer privacy.* Paper presented at the meeting of the Association for Education in Journalism and Mass Communication, Boston, MA.

Office of Technology Assessment. (1988). *Criminal justice, new technologies and the Constitution.* Washington, DC: U.S. Government Printing Office.

Post, R. (1989). The social foundations of privacy: Community and self in the common law tort. *California Law Review, 77*, 957–1010.

Rawls, J. (1971). *A theory of justice.* Cambridge, MA: Harvard University Press.

Rawls, J. (1985). Justice as fairness: Political not metaphysical. *Philosophy & Public Affairs, 14*, 223–251.

Ready to zero in on census data. (1991, January 28). *Advertising Age*, p. 16.

Spencer, D. (1985). When a record goes into the computer. *The IRE Journal*, p. 6.

Stricharchuk, G. (1988, February 3). Computer records become powerful tool for investigative reporters and editors. *The Wall Street Journal*, p. 25.

Strnad, P. (1990, December 10). Count on cartography. *Advertising Age*, p. 46.

Thomson, J. (1984). The right to privacy. In F. Schoeman (Ed.), *Philosophical dimensions of privacy: An anthology* (pp. 272–289). Cambridge, UK: Cambridge University Press.

Walker, R. (1990, September 25). Computer data bases can be valuable sources. *The Christian Science Monitor*, p. 14.

Journal of Mass Media Ethics
Vol. 9, No. 4, pp. 243–256

Bringing Communication Technology Under Ethical Analysis: A Case Study of Newspaper Audiotex

By George Albert Gladney
University of Illinois at Urbana–Champaign

❏*This study uses dialogic theory and philosophy of technology to provide an ethical framework for analysis of newspaper audiotex, or electronic voice information services. It concludes that growth of newspaper audiotex (a) is bound by notions of technological determinism and the technological imperative, (b) is driven by virtuosity values related more to personal aggrandizement of its developers than concern for consequences in the user sphere, and (c) signifies a shift in newspapers' communicative stance with readers to monologic mode emphasizing power/persuasion. Consequences for the coming of the electronic newspaper are considered.*

Mass media scholar and ethicist Clifford Christians (1989) observed that the "technological system we call the mass media has been understood from an ethical viewpoint," astutely adding that "only in rudimentary form to date have technologies themselves been brought under ethical analysis" (p. 243). Although ethical analysis has focused on such things as the New World Information Order and privacy issues, much of it has concentrated on media functions—news, advertising, entertainment—not particular technologies. Given the lack of a systematic, integrative approach for ethical assessment of communications technologies, Christians urged that we look to both communications theory, particularly dialogic theory, and philosophy of technology.

Taking Christians's plea seriously, this study treats newspaper audiotex ("voice information services," or voice/electronic data messaging) as a case study. Audiotex (or audiotext) is chosen because it is a "cutting edge" technology precursory to the electronic, or "paperless," newspaper. Audiotex is a key development because it (a) gives newspapers experience with electronic delivery of information; (b) alters the communicative stance between newspaper and reader; (c) allows readers to circumvent exposure to uninteresting parts of the paper; (d) allows the newspaper to learn more about readers' needs, wants, and opinions; and (e) fosters less direct communication between the paper and its readers through mediation of systems that recognize, synthesize, store, and retrieve the human voice. These effects may be greatly extended and magnified with the electronic newspaper.

The term *newspaper audiotex* refers to interactive, computerized services in which readers call the newspaper or an 800 or 900 number to deliver or receive voice information, thus, the terms "talking newspaper," "voice information services," and "telepress." Audiotex typically involves voice-mail technology that depends on conversion of the human voice from analog signals, which are proportional to changes in electrical voltage, into digital code—the familiar 1's and 0's that computers use to talk to each other—so that the voice can be "processed like so much electronic sausage" (Ramirez, 1992, p. III-9).

There are two types of audiotex services: sponsor paid and caller paid (Potter, 1991a). With the first type, the newspaper advertises a number a reader can call to get a particular category of information: weather, sports scores, stock quotations, lottery results, soap opera summaries, movie/book reviews, horoscopes, and so forth. Before receiving the desired information, callers hear a promotional message from the newspaper or an advertiser. The second type involves three-digit (800, 900, and 976) services in which revenues are shared by the newspaper, telephone company, and sometimes providers of syndicated material (Potter, 1991a; M. Smith, 1991). Audiotex also is used for personal ads, subscriptions, letter dictation, instant reader polls, and so forth. (DiSante, 1992a, 1992b; Fitzgerald, 1992b; Weiner, 1992).

To bring newspaper audiotex technology under ethical analysis, this case study attempts to explicate an acceptable rationale by which to discuss norms linked to communication technology. The study seeks illumination from philosophy of technology and borrows from dialogic theory as a transition to ethics. It relies heavily on the philosophy of technology articulated by Arnold Pacey and several scholars with close conceptual affinity to Pacey—Manfred Stanley, Jacques Ellul, and Martin Heidegger. Turning to dialogic theory, the study cites the work of Martin Buber, Ivan Illich, Clifford Christians, Jacques Ellul, Floyd Matson, and Ashley Montagu.

This article begins by outlining relevant theoretical and philosophical contributions of these scholars; those contributions then are applied to an analysis of newspaper audiotex. Method of analysis is qualitative, involving review of many dozens of articles and commentaries appearing in newspaper trade and professional publications and a few general interest publications. The study concludes by assessing ethical implications of newspaper audiotex and extending the analysis to the electronic newspaper.

Contribution of Philosophy of Technology

The idea that technology is value free is widely accepted, Pacey (1983) argued, because values incorporated into technological products and the process of design and manufacture are unrecognized or simply taken for granted. "People have come to feel that technological development proceeds independently of human purpose," wrote Pacey, "they see it as the working out of a rational pattern based on impersonal logic" (p. 78). The common view accepts progress as one-dimensional, linear; it accepts a technological determinism that "presents technical advance as a process of steady development dragging human society along in its train" (p. 24). The motto: "Science finds—Industry applies—Man conforms" (p. 25).

Progress is seen as coming in cycles or "waves," too. Pacey warned that historical analysis that seeks to identify "patterns and rhythms in development" (p. 31) may become deterministic (implying that processes are at work that no human intervention can alter). We accept that technical advance is the leading edge of progress; each era is associated with succeeding technologies. Today we live in the computer age or nuclear age; earlier it was the steam age, iron age, and so forth. This technical progress, Pacey asserted, is thought to bring social evolution in its wake.

It follows, according to Pacey (1983), that technical development is left in the hands of "experts," technical people with the right know-how. The implication: We may dislike the idea of nuclear power or heart transplant surgery but "we have to solve the technical problems connected with these things if engineering and medicine are to develop" (p. 26). In other words, we cannot stop technology. For Pacey, this mindset is part of the "technological imperative"—"the lure of always pushing toward the greatest feat of technical performance or complexity" (p. 79). It is the view that "whatever is feasible must always be tried" (p. 79). Yet Pacey, warned that the perception of technical progress as "autonomous" and "irresistible" masks unquestioning acceptance of economic values or promotion for the sake of prestige and political gain. Thus we have moon exploration and "Star Wars" defense systems—damn the costs.

Pacey (1983) drew our attention to the "existential" joys of engineering, or what he called the "virtuosity values" (p. 81)—values that arise from basic human impulses such as love of speed or power or sport. Thus, development of the hydrogen bomb was so "technically sweet" (p. 81), it simply had to be developed. Pacey would have us replace or offset virtuosity values with "user values" (p. 102) more closely attuned to basic human needs and welfare. Technology should be driven by concern for what people need, not what professionals can supply. We need an ethical discipline that deals with conflicts between values in the expert sphere and the user sphere.

Stanley (1978) argued that until humankind revitalizes the notion of human dignity, it will lack a standard to judge the morality of the technological enterprise. The problem is the sacralizing of the technological motif and the saturating of our language with technicist metaphors from machineness. For Stanley, "technicism" (p. 12) is the illegitimate dominance of scientific and technological reasoning over other interpretations of human existence. Stanley called for recovery of our language from the dominance of "experts" and their technicist talk, and he urges that human dignity become society's animating force.

Ellul (1977/1980), too, complains of machineness, *la technique*. He warned of the technological mystique that supremely values machinelike efficiency. Ellul saw technology as alienating and self-augmenting, taking on a life of its own. He observed that technology "does not tolerate being halted for a moral reason" (p. 147); too often thought is not given to its ultimate human purpose. Ellul lamented lack of a systematic, integrative approach to bring technologies themselves under ethical analysis. He stated that "man in our society has no intellectual, moral, or spiritual reference point for judging and criticizing technology" (p. 318).

Heidegger (1954/1977) asserted that when technology is professionalized or commandeered for an aim other than to fulfill our lives with purpose and virtue, when it is distorted into the domain of power, it is repressive and dehumanizing. Heidegger and Stanley were concerned that there is something about the technological process that leads us to accept removal of the human agent from that process, so that humans sacrifice their humanity for a "larger" cause. Thus, we come to worship the destining of the technological process, so that once technology is in place, expansion of the process is accepted uncritically.

Contribution of Dialogic Theory

For Buber (1967, 1970), the essence of ethics is found in true dialogue (an "I–Thou" relationship), not moral codes of conduct. As Griffin (1991) explained, truth comes from "spontaneous transparency of self with others, whereas warped communication puts all of its energy into 'seeming'"; if one desires genuine dialogue, one will concentrate instead on "being" (pp. 365–366).

For Buber (1967), genuine dialogue exists when "each of the participants really has in mind the other or others in their present and particular being and turns to them with the intention of establishing a living mutual relation between himself and them" (p. 113). He distinguished genuine dialogue from "technical dialogue" prompted by the need of objective understanding, and "monologue disguised as dialogue" (p. 113), that is, "when a man withdraws from accepting with his essential being another person in his particularity" (p. 117). The basic movement of dialogue, conversely, is "the turn towards the other," not only physically but in "requisite measure with the soul" (p. 115).

Christians (1988) took Buber to mean that "we ourselves live humanly when we accept others with unconditional positive regard" (p. 18). Noting Buber's famous line, "in the beginning is the relation," Christians claimed that Buber intended that statement ontologically, "as a category of being." Thus, the "relational reality"—the reciprocal bond, the person as interpersonal—is an "irreducible anthropological phenomenon" (p. 18).

Dialogic theory helps discern values imbedded in communication technologies. Matson and Montagu (1967), for example, argued that the monologic approach, seeing communication as "the transmission and reception of symbolic stimuli (messages or commands), finds its classical formulation in the art and science of rhetoric and its characteristic modern expressions in cybernetics, combative game theory, and the repertoires of mass persuasion" (p. viii). The dialogic approach, conversely, "regards communication as the path to communion and the ground of self-discovery" (p. viii).

Christians (1988) stated that the monologic (I–It) mode is in the imperative mood, best fit for control systems; communication systems reflecting this model thus are seen as "transmission belts" or behavioristic or electrical systems carrying stimuli with the intent of eliciting responses. Carey (1989) has criticized this model—what he called the "power" or "anxiety" model—because it fosters a view of society as a political order (network of power, administration, decision, control), or, alternatively, an economic order (relations of property, production, and trade) (p. 34).

Illich's (1973) important contribution is his notion of "convivial" technology. Technology is convivial if it (a) maintains "natural scales and limits" (p. xxiv) and (b) opposes the ends of mere "industrial production" (p. 12). But, to be convivial, the political process must govern establishment and control of technology. Tools must permit "autonomous and creative intercourse" (p. 12) among persons; tools are anticonvivial when linked to conditioned responses or associated with demands of a man-made environment. For Illich, conviviality is "individual freedom realized in personal interdependence and, as such, an intrinsic ethical value" (p. 11).

Illich shared Stanley's urging that we reclaim language from dominance of experts' technicist talk. As Pauly (1983) explained, a convivial society for Illich "begins with an intelligible language of action not dominated by professional abstractions but rooted in the shared experiences of everyday life" (p. 265).

The Paceyan and dialogic perspectives supremely value the Judeo–Christian moral command to love God and humankind. They resonate with *agape*, which Christians, Rotzoll, and Fackler (1991) defined as "unselfish, other-regarding care and other-directed love" (pp. 19–20) and rejection of giving others only instrumental values.

Paceyan Perspectives

A review of the trade press reveals that much of the newspaper industry sees expansion of audiotex as inevitable, part of the playing out of the impersonal logic and autonomous progression of technological development. One writer, for example, declared that audiotex is part of publishers' "inexorable drive to Information Age sophistication," adding that "no doubt tomorrow's technology is fast approaching" (Buckman, 1991, p. 8TC). One pictures a train approaching with humankind anxiously awaiting to jump aboard, not sure where it is headed but trusting that it will lead to progress. Another writer, noting how audiotex allows new ways for reporters to collect data, stated that this change in the journalistic process is "*mandated by* [italics added] technological changes" (Manshel, 1993, pp. 12TC, 19TC) that compress time and reward computer literacy. Still another writer proclaimed: "Telecommunications for newspapers is a door opener, a way to do things differently, but also a way to do things [they have] never done before. To boldly go—wherever" (Conniff, 1993d, p. 21TC). The implication: There is intrinsic value in doing things differently. Expectation of constant change is consonant with the technological imperative that guides progress. Whatever is feasible must be tried, even when we don't have the faintest idea where it is taking us.

The trade press is replete with metaphors suggesting audiotex is the next "wave" or "generation" of evolutionary or revolutionary advance for newspapers (Fitzgerald, 1992a, 1992c; "Newspapers Offering," 1992). One writer observed that audiotex presages "the dawn of New Age Journalism" (M. Smith, 1991, p. 2TC). Another gushed that with audiotex newspapers are "in the thrall of a spell that will touch us all before the decade is out," adding that audiotex portends "an explosion of media exploration unprecedented in the history of any medium" (Conniff, 1993a, p. 4TC).

Although many writers claim that newspaper adoption of audiotex stems from fear of competition from the regional Bell operating companies ("Attack," 1991; Fitzgerald, 1991; Potter, 1991b), others warn that, even without that competition, newspaper audiotex and diversification of information delivery systems is inevitable, like the playing out of some autonomous, irresistible force. Typical is a newspaper chain executive's assertion that newspapers that try to block the telephone industry from providing information services are "spitting into the winds of change that technology has wrought rather than harnessing those winds to sail on into the new world of information distribution" (Gersh, 1992, p. 7). Notice it is change that technology has wrought—suggestive of technical advance, to borrow Pacey's (1983) phrase, "as a process of steady development dragging human society along in its train" (p. 24).

The spread of audiotex suggests the working out of a technological imperative that masks unquestioning acceptance of economic values (revenues/profits) and subordination of concern for basic human needs. For one thing, it means advertising messages go in front of news/information instead of adjacent to it. Unlike readers of the traditional newspaper, audiotex listeners cannot completely ignore or avoid exposure to commercial messages accompanying editorial copy. An executive of a midsize New York daily observed that, done well, audiotex can be very profitable with advertising sponsorship. Addressing an industry panel, the executive urged that a commercial be played on every message to get listeners used to the idea of advertising. "Otherwise," he said, "when you introduce ads, callers will be irritated by the intrusion" (Stein, 1993, p. 16). This creeping commercialism can come in double doses with audiotex. One paper in Pennsylvania, for example, offers a 900-WeatherTrak service in which callers listen to a pharmacy advertisement at the beginning of the call and additionally pay 75 cents the first minute—in effect, paying to listen to the commercial message (M. Smith, 1991, p. 3TC).

Rapid growth of audiotex has spawned a new trade magazine, *Newspapers & Voice,* and its columns, not surprisingly, reflect boundless enthusiasm for the technology and bright prospect for profits. For example, the magazine's editor wrote that voice personal ads "can provide a steady pay-per-call revenue stream about the size of the Mississippi River" (Weiner, 1992, p. 19). With a successful voice personals service, he continued, "the money is rolling in and readers—not to mention those who wield sharp pencils in the controller's office—are happy" (p. 21). Similarly, an audiotex provider executive explained that many of his newspaper clients "have a tendency to come to us once they start running voice personals and start receiving their checks and say, 'This is fantastic! What else do you have?'" (p. 21). The concern, it seems, is with what professionals can supply, not what people need.

Audiotex developers have produced a lexicon that promotes a technicist aura about the whole enterprise. Even the name audiotex, with the affix "tex" (sounded as in "techs"), adds to this effect. One writer complained of "audiotex techno-babel"—jargon such as "navigation systems," "ANI," and "PIN-plus database management" (Fitzgerald, 1992c, p. 14). Another writer—awed by terms such as "audiotex," "voice capture," "automated attendance systems," and "unusual abbreviations like 'IVR' for 'Voice Response Systems'"— observed that "whenever computers are involved in a development, normal vocabulary goes out the window" (DeYoung, 1992, p. 4TC).

Audiotex is placed with digital photography and electronic pagination on the cutting-edge of newspaper technology (Potter, 1993). These developments presumably demonstrate that papers have shed their traditional aversion to change (Conniff, 1993a). Toward that end it must please editors to see technicist headlines such as these in 1992 *Newspapers & Voice*: "SpectraFAX Introduces Liaison Data Connectivity Products," "Speaker-Independent Voice Recognition Available for Hello! System," and "Innovative Technology Debuts Voice Perfect Audioforms."

Still, one can get carried away with hyperbole and gee-wizardry connected with the technology. As one newspaper executive explained, "All an audiotex system does is simply convert analog signals to digital and store the information on a disc. So, we got some answering machine software at the store and played with it. This isn't rocket science" (Potter, 1991a, p. 12).

Perhaps audiotex is made to seem more complicated than it is in order to create a technicist aura and to stress the fact that the technology is in the hands of experts with specialized knowledge. Viewed in that context, the technicist talk becomes a means to shut out any questions or objections from nonexperts. If we heed Stanley, Heidegger, and Illich we will see the creation of technicist terms as a way of commandeering and professionalizing the technology and perverting its use for the sake of power, prestige, and political/economic gain—not human welfare, fulfillment, and dignity. Or, using Pacey's schema, we will see technicist talk as saturating the expert sphere, where virtuosity values reign over user values.

Dialogic Perspectives

One great paradox of audiotex is that it makes the newspaper a more personal object, more closely attuned to readers' individual interests, yet at the same time depersonalizes relations with customers by substituting synthetic communication for communication via the written word (letters to the paper) or direct and interpersonal (talking to a newspaper representative, live, on the telephone). Although acknowledging that customers prefer live operators, telephone companies converted to voice-automated services to cut costs. The same pressure is said to drive audiotex because eliminating live operators reduces payrolls (Davis, 1992; Langer, 1990).

Dialogic theory helps us sort out this paradox and provides ethical insight when we realize that audiotex counters genuine dialogue in several ways. Audiotex involves voice recognition systems that constrain free-flowing speech. Voice information systems, for example, typically involve a guided question-and-answer path that takes the caller to the relevant information, and the confined, closed-end nature of the experience can be frustrating. Callers complain of being captured in "voice-mail jail," described by one writer as "that labyrinth of recorded voices issuing instructions from which there sometimes seems no escape short of hanging up" (Ramirez, 1992, p. 9). One complainer called voice mail "a telephone form of Chinese water torture" and "voice mail from hell" (Davis, 1992, p. 12). Discrete voice recognition requires callers to pause briefly between each spoken command from the robotic voice for confirmation ("Speaker-Independent," 1992). Speech synthesis software converts electronic or fax text to a "natural-sounding" female voice, but the voice only "seems" natural ("Sound Bytes," 1992). Actually, the voice of voice mail (the "automated attendant" or "robot switchboard") is usually that of a woman (an employee of voice-mail equipment makers) whose voice is prized for its friendly, yet authoritative, persona. Messages are assembled from separately recorded sound bites spliced together as if they were spoken.

All of this shows how audiotex applies to Ellul's notion of alienation, disconnectedness, and the dehumanizing aspect of machineness. Certainly it relates to Heidegger's and Stanley's concern that there is something about the technological process that leads to removal of humans from the process, understood in terms of efficiency. One phone executive explained:

"It's inevitable that everyone's going to computerized voices. It's cost-saving. It's more efficient" (Langer, 1990, p. H3).

A further point to consider is that consumers are prone to accept this new technology, despite their complaints. The slogan noted earlier, "Science finds—Industry applies—Man conforms,"does not rule out the possibility that although humans conform, they may grumble about the change. But there is never any doubt that, given time, we will adapt to the new technology. Audiotex promoters tell the story of the answering machine; at first, use of the device was considered antisocial, but today it is considered antisocial not to have one (Langer, 1990; Markoff, 1990).

Audiotex also alters the newspaper's relationship with the community. An executive with Knight–Ridder newspapers confided that audiotex's down side is loss of "the personal touch." At some smaller papers, he explained, "the same operator would be on the console for 10 to 15 years. She knew everybody and served almost like a help desk" (Davis, 1992, p. 13). Now, with audiotex, readers call the newspaper late at night, when no one is in the building, and communicate. The personnel talk of "24-hour capture" of letters to the editor and information about funerals, obituaries, weddings, and so forth (Todd, 1992). They do not have to deal interpersonally, directly, with any individual bearing this information.

Audiotex affects newsroom operations, too. First, reporters do interviews without talking to the interviewee. This is accomplished by leaving questions on the interviewee's voice mail and retrieving the reply after the interviewee has left answers in the reporter's voice mailbox (Davis, 1992). Audiotex experts call this "mailbox conversation" and contrast it with "real-time conversation," or live, spontaneous, communication as in a conventional telephone conversation (Weatherford, 1993). Second, newsrooms are encouraged to use data-base computer technology provided by audiotex to conduct and report reader surveys on a variety of issues.

These developments suggest newspapers are, in Buber's way of thinking, taking a turn away from their readers, physically and in terms of the soul. There seems to be no sense of a living, mutual relation between humans at the newspaper and individual readers.

Moreover, audiotex has generated little enthusiasm among newsroom staffers and subeditors. Articles about audiotex usually are found in journals aimed at newspaper executive suites. Except for providing instant reader polls and sparing reporters the burden of gathering routine information (weddings, calendar, etc.) via telephone, audiotex simply doesn't benefit the newsroom.

Another factor for the newsroom is the dubious news value of audiotex "information." For example, top audiotex features provided by one medium-size Iowa paper are dog racing, horoscope, lottery, soap opera updates, sports, stock market, trivia quiz, and weather (Debth, 1992). This sort of fare is rarely called news in audiotex circles; the euphemism "news enhancement" is favored (Stein, 1993). Not surprisingly, a paper's audiotex director typically has a marketing/advertising background, or is a subeditor borrowed from the newsroom to lend an air of legitimacy to the paper's audiotex effort (Kelsey, 1992; M. Smith, 1991). In sum, marketers, not news specialists, are promoting audiotex. Nowhere is that made more clear than in *Editor & Publisher's* annual telecommunications issue; essentially all nonadvertising copy is produced by audiotex consultants, most of whom have a vested interest in the technology.

Marketing people adore audiotex partly because it permits the newspaper, much like its direct-mail and shared-mail competitors, to precisely target advertising to specific readers. One large Midwestern daily, for example, pitches audiotex to advertisers by distributing an information kit that pledges: "Every dollar you invest hits the target!" The kit stresses that a "captive audience" hears the ad before receiving the requested data (Stein, 1993).

This sort of rationale fits squarely in the monologic mode because it embraces a technology for purposes of control and persuasion and, ultimately, economic or political gain. One is reminded of the "I–It" modality implicit in the cybernetic, or behavioristic, or power-anxiety model. (It is not mere coincidence that audiotechies are fond of the word "capture.")

Summary and Afterword

This study leaves one with a strong sense that newspaper audiotex enthusiasts adhere to a technological determinism that deeply reflects virtuosity values and the technological imperative.

The technology is driven by what professionals can supply; there is fascination and allure of the "technically sweet" and achievement of maximum technical complexity and performance. Furthermore, the technicist language of audiotex (a) reminds us that experts are in charge of development, and (b) contributes to a state of mind that precludes legitimation of any reasoning or interpretation other than the technical. This distancing from language rooted in the shared experience of everyday life is one more way audiotex disjoins the user sphere.

This study shows in several ways how audiotex opposes the movement of "I–Thou" dialogue and alters the communicative stance and bond between newspaper and community. With voice recognition/synthesis systems, audiotex removes us several steps from live, direct, spontaneous communication between newspaper and reader. For the sake of efficiency, we accept removal of the human agent from the process. This is, in Buber's phrase, a turn away from the other physically and in terms of the soul.

This "turning away" fits the monologic ("I–It") mode, with its emphasis on seeming (rather than being) and technical dialogue cued by the need for objective understanding. In many cases audiotex is linked to power/persuasion goals of the newspaper and advertisers—not to convivial goals of filling lives with purpose and virtue and providing the grounds of communion and self-discovery.

The newspaper industry generally sees audiotex as one more step in a process of steady progress. Whether it sees this technical advance as the working out of a rational pattern based on an impersonal logic is difficult to say, but it seems likely. That is because, as A. Smith (1986) reminded us, designers of all present newspaper technology systems accept the idea of an ultimate system employing "paperless" or electronic technology. That system depends on conversion of all analog signals to digital. With conversion complete, the electronic newspaper will be linked to a vast, global network of digitized "information highways" interfaced with various display forms (audio, video, print, etc.). Audiotex is merely one step in the conversion. Thus, experience gained with electronic delivery is the reason newspapers commonly cite for adopting audiotex (Kelsey, 1993). This preparation for the inevitable illustrates Heidegger's point that once the technology is in place, expansion of the process tends to be accepted uncritically.

Because audiotex is intermediary to the electronic newspaper, we should bear in mind two crucial biases of audiotex technology: (a) its interactive potential for buildup of reader–subscriber–customer data bases, and (b) its ability to fragment and customize presentation of news and entertainment according to individual tastes. How newspapers handle this new capacity tells us much about what to expect with the electronic or "paperless" newspaper.

There are two models for the electronic newspaper: the browse model and target model. The browse model assumes readers prefer news organized and edited by news organizations. One prominent designer envisions a tablet-sized computer that will produce a newspaper page on the screen. With the tap of a pen and menu commands, readers can scan any and all content, much as with conventional ink-on-paper technology (Markoff, 1992).

With the target model, readers specify a custom package of news, entertainment, and advertising. As time passes, the system's interactive nature permits the paper to monitor reading patterns, construct a profile of readers' interests, and fine tune content selection (Barker, 1992; Conniff, 1993b, 1993d; Jennewein, 1991; Kerwin, 1992). Thus the target model is heralded as the "personal newspaper" (Conniff, 1993b, 1993c).

What is alarming about newspaper audiotex is that it points toward acceptance of the target model and its emphasis on giving readers only what they want (or expect), and data-base buildup for more efficient marketing and persuasion. Bogart (in Freedom Forum Media Studies Center, 1993) observed that with the target model "more information is acquired intentionally and less serendipitously" (p. 11). This means less of a role for professionals who package information. Placing news judgment in the hands of professionals may sound distinctly monological and anticonvivial, but Bogart points out correctly that without someone to select, package, measure, and label information, it becomes random and chaotic and produces mental indigestion. Bogart (1990) added importantly, "Editors have to know what readers will tolerate, but their job is to push up constantly against the limits of that tolerance and thus to expand it" (p. 60).

With the target model the electronic newspaper can tailor news to suit so-called "communities of the mind" (Freedom Forum Media Studies Center, 1993, p. 21). One news package for White supremacists, another for African Americans; one for realists, another for escapists; one for internationalists, another for isolationists. Missing is news that any or all of these groups wish not to be confronted with, but which nonetheless has important bearing on the welfare of the geographic community or polity. Missing is what Nord (1985) would describe as a newspaper that assumes great interdependence among diverse city dwellers and reflects the collective life of the city—a newspaper that articulates a vision of public community, urges a community spirit, and provides readers with a limited, organized, common frame of reference. Instead, with the target model, a paper is private in outlook and individualistic in focus, seeing the community as a fragmented assortment of private affairs. For those of us concerned about the media's contribution to so-called "eclipse of community," the target model is a negative foreboding.

References

Attack of the baby bells. (1991, October 26). *Editor & Publisher*, p. 4.

Barker, M. (1992). Newspoint 2010. *Newspapers & Voice*, 4(4), 16.

Bogart, L. (1990, December). In pondering the customized newspaper, don't lose sight of big picture. *Presstime*, p. 60.

Buber, M. (1967). Between man and man: The realms. In F. Matson & A. Montagu (Eds.), *The human dialogue* (pp. 113–117). New York: Free Press.

Buber, M. (1970). *I and thou* (W. Kaufmann, Trans.). New York: Scribner's.

Buckman, J. (1991, January 26). Buckle your seat belt; this trip has just begun. *Editor & Publisher*, pp. 8TC, 25TC.

Carey, J. (1989). *Communication as culture*. Boston: Unwin Hyman.

Christians, C. (1988). Dialogic communication theory and cultural studies. *Studies in Symbolic Interaction*, 9, 3–31.

Christians, C. (1989). Communications technology: An assessment of the literature. In F. Ferre & C. Mitcham (Eds.), *Research in philosophy and technology: Ethics and technology* (pp. 233–249). Greenwich, CT: JAI Press.

Christians, C., Rotzoll, K., & Fackler, M. (1991). *Media ethics* (3rd ed.). New York: Longman.

Conniff, M. (1993a, March 6). The dinosaur is starting to dance. *Editor & Publisher*, pp. 4TC, 6TC.

Conniff, M. (1993b, January 16). Enter the personal newspaper. *Editor & Publisher*, p. 3.

Conniff, M. (1993c, March 6). In search of the personal newspaper. *Editor & Publisher*, pp. 15TC, 18TC.

Conniff, M. (1993d, March 6). Where are we going? Newspapers and the new interactive technologies. *Editor & Publisher*, pp. 8TC, 10TC–11TC.

Davis, N. (1992, April). Newspapers sort the pros and cons of voice mail. *Editor & Publisher*, pp. 12–13.

Debth, J. (1992, February 1). How *Cedar Rapids Gazette* uses power of "telepress" for growth. *Editor & Publisher*, pp. 6TC, 8TC.

DeYoung, B. (1992, February 1). A layman's view of "telepress." *Editor & Publisher*, p. 4TC.

DiSante, E. (1992a). The pricing pickle. *Newspapers & Technology*, 4(5), 21.

DiSante, E. (1992b). Romancing bottom line. *Newspapers & Technology*, 4(5), 1, 19.

Ellul, J. (1980). *The technological system* (J. Neugroschel, Trans.). New York: Seabury Continuum. (Original work published 1977)

Fitzgerald, M. (1991, October 12). Collision course. *Editor & Publisher*, pp. 12–13.

Fitzgerald, M. (1992a, February 22). The future of audiotex for newspapers. *Editor & Publisher*, pp. 15, 35.

Fitzgerald, M. (1992b, February 15). Wake-up call: Newspaper audiotex ringing up dollars in bad economic times. *Editor & Publisher*, pp. 16–17, 43.

Fitzgerald, M. (1992c, February 22). What do callers think? Focus group evaluates prototype audiotex service. *Editor & Publisher*, p. 14.

Freedom Forum Media Studies Center. (1993). *Media, democracy, and the information highway*. New York: Author.

Gersh, D. (1992, March 28). Neuharth pulls no punches. *Editor & Publisher*, pp. 7–8.

Griffin, E. (1991). *A first look at communication theory*. New York: McGraw-Hill.

Heidegger, M. (1977). *The question concerning technology and other essays* (W. Lovitt, Trans.). New York: Harper & Row. (Original work published 1954)

Illich, I. (1973). *Tools for conviviality*. New York: Harper & Row.

Jennewein, C. (1991, January 26). U.S. in the forefront of new technologies. *Editor & Publisher*, pp. 10TC, 28TC.

Kelsey, J., III. (1992, February 1). 24 hard-earned lessons of talking newspapers. *Editor & Publisher*, p. 15TC.

Kelsey, J., III. (1993, March 6). A future in electronic services. *Editor & Publisher*, p. 16TC.

Kerwin, A. (1992, November 21). Electronic newspaper of the future. *Editor & Publisher*, pp. 28–29.

Langer, G. (1990, February 11). Computers reach out, respond to human voice. *The Washington Post*, p. H3.

Manshel, D. (1993, March 6). Data bases empower news/ad departments. *Editor & Publisher*, pp. 12TC, 19TC.

Markoff, J. (1990, December 23). Another way to get to the global village. *The New York Times*, p. E-6.

Markoff, J. (1992, June 28). A media pioneer's quest: Portable electronic newspapers. *The New York Times*, p. III-11.

Matson, F., & Montagu, A. (1967). Preface. In F. Matson & A. Montagu (Eds.), *The human dialogue* (pp. vii–ix). New York: Free Press.

Newspapers offering the latest news by phone. (1992, November 9). *Publishers' Auxiliary*, p. 11.

Nord, D. (1985). The public community: The urbanization of journalism in Chicago. *Journal of Urban History*, 11, 411–441.

Pacey, A. (1983). *The culture of technology*. Cambridge, MA: MIT Press.

Pauly, J. (1983). Ivan Illich and mass communications studies. *Communication Research*, *10*, 259–280.

Potter, W. (1991a, July). How to build your own audiotex system. *Presstime*, pp. 10–12.

Potter, W. (1991b, September). Newspapers prepare for competition with RBOCs. *Presstime*, pp. 16–21.

Potter, W. (1993, January). Big ideas: America's small dailies are putting progressive thinking to the test. *Presstime*, pp. 39–44.

Ramirez, A. (1992, May 3). From the voice mail acorn, a still-spreading oak. *The New York Times*, p. III-9.

Smith, A. (1986). *Goodbye Gutenberg: The newspaper revolution of the 1980s*. New York: Oxford University Press.

Smith, M. (1991, January 26). New age journalism. *Editor & Publisher*, p. 2TC.

Sound Bytes lets you listen to faxes, e–mail. (1992, May). *Newspapers & Voice*, p. 36.

Speaker–independent voice recognition available for Hello! system. (1992, May). *Newspapers & Voice*, p. 35.

Stanley, M. (1978). *The technological conscience*. Chicago: University of Chicago Press.

Stein, M. (1993, January 9). Ideas on audiotex. *Editor & Publisher*, pp. 16, 18.

Todd, A. (1992, November 9). How one paper got into electronic information. *Publishers' Auxiliary*, p. 13.

Weatherford, D. (1993, March 6). New PIN product. *Editor & Publisher*, p. 6TC.

Weiner, A. (1992, May). Adventures in talking ads. *Newspapers & Voice*, pp. 19–21, 25.

Journal of Mass Media Ethics
Vol. 9, No. 4, pp. 257–266

Cases and Commentaries

The *Journal of Mass Media Ethics* publishes case studies in which scholars and media professionals outline how they would address a particular ethical problem. Some cases are purely hypothetical, but most are from actual experience in newsrooms, corporations, and other agencies.

We invite readers to call our attention to current cases and issues. We also invite suggestions of names of people, both professionals and academicians, who might write commentaries.

I wrote the following case in consultation with Jack Shafer, editor of *Washington City Paper*, and Robert Ellis Smith, publisher of *Privacy Journal*, Providence, RI.

Lou Hodges
Washington and Lee University
Lexington, VA 24450
(703) 463-8786

Should Videotape Rentals Be Private?

During the 1988 Senate confirmation hearings on Robert Bork's nomination to the U.S. Supreme Court, *Washington City Paper*, a Washington, DC weekly, received from a videotape rental store a list of titles showing Bork's videotape rentals. The newspaper published the story, including the list, while the hearings were going on.

Bork had testified that the U.S. Constitution affords no protection of privacy. It was in that spirit, said Jack Shafer, editor of *Washington City Paper*, that the video store volunteered the list to a reporter, and in the same spirit the newspaper published it.

The thinking at the paper was that, given his views on the Constitution and privacy, surely Bork would not mind publication of this arguably private information. There was nothing shocking about the titles he had rented, and editors had no doubt about the authenticity of the information or of its source.

Several senators denounced the paper for publishing the story, and Congress soon passed what is often referred to as the "Bork Bill" (The Video Privacy Protection Act, 18 U.S.C § 2710, 1988), a law designed to prevent unauthorized release of specific titles rented by identifiable individuals. The law does allow rental agencies to reveal general categories of topics a person has chosen. Nothing in the statute relates to publication by a news organization; the focus is on rental agencies.

With the advent of new technologies for spreading information, we are likely to encounter with increasing frequency opportunities for journalists to obtain private information about individuals. Marketing departments within news organizations, for example, already have data for "targeting" purposes. Looking into the future, which promises even greater capacity to obtain private information about individuals, what kinds of guidelines do we need? As a focus for that question, consider the following situation in light of the Bork case.

Suppose that, having been promised anonymity, a sales clerk at a video-tape rental agency gave a reporter friend a 2-year record of specific titles rented by an incumbent male senator who is up for reelection. The list included *Debbie Does Dallas* and some well-known pedophillic titles. You, as editor, along with a dozen or so others, received the list on Internet. By good fortune you also obtained, legally, a public library listing of books the senator has borrowed, a list that includes titles that would be of interest to the sizable "religious right" in your state.

What issues should you confront and what questions should you ask yourself in deciding whether and how to proceed?

Commentary #1

Damned if You Do, Damned if You Don't

Once again, the demon media are faced with a damned-if-you-do, damned-if-you-don't scenario.

If we run with this story, the senator will deny all, accuse us of tabloid journalism, insist we have a political agenda, and maybe even sue for libel. Not to mention that we'll be setting the right to privacy back several pegs.

On the other hand, if word is out that the newspaper was a recipient of this information and chose to remain silent, we'll be accused of covering up for the incumbent candidate, denying the public its right to know, and possibly even endangering the lives of innocent children who may cross the senator's path.

It won't be the first or last time a newspaper has had to make a difficult decision. Here are some of the issues that I think need to be considered:

1. *The Law. Debbie Does Dallas* may be a porno classic, but pedophillia is something else. Does the good senator just watch Nabokov's *Lolita* (a shocker back in 1962 but pretty humdrum by today's standards), or is he getting his jollies from the hard-core stuff with child actors? Under state law, it is a felony to produce, distribute, or exhibit pedophillic material. Although it may not be against the law to view such material, it would certainly put pressure on the newspaper to reveal the senator's viewing habits if he were paying to rent such XXX-rated fare.

2. *Right to Privacy.* With the growing loss of privacy because of electronic access, new standards of journalism are needed—or the old ones need some dusting off and rethinking. If we snoop into a person's reading

and viewing habits, can we peer into his or her bedroom, checkbook, or credit cards? Are there limits we're putting to data-base access—to electronic bulletin-board revelations? How do they apply in this case?

3. *Across-the-Board Fairness.* Almost by chance, we have a list of videos rented by the incumbent senator. What about the other candidates— shouldn't their video vagaries also be uncovered? Under the "Bork Bill," we can ask the video stores to give us general topics, but no titles. So do we ask the candidates to voluntarily make this information available, or do we just live with the likelihood that we cannot tell our readers what videos candidates X, Y, and Z watched?

4. *Public's Right to Know.* Are the senator's "sleazy" videos and books for his own viewing pleasure, or research for legislation? Maybe, just maybe, the good senator is an upright member of the Senate subcommittee for banning pornographic movies and books. On the other hand, if the videos and books are strictly for personal fun and games, does the senator pose a physical or moral threat to his constituency? I'd put that question to the experts—criminologists, psychologists, and so forth. But either way, does the electorate have a right to know and draw its own conclusions?

5. *Motive and Timing.* The election is coming up. Does the "anonymous" source have a political motive for the revelations? In other words, is our video salesclerk a member of the opposition party with a grudge against the incumbent, or just a celebrity watcher who recognized the customer and got queasy at the senator's viewing tastes? Also, the newspaper will be accused of trying to swing votes away from the senator. Can the paper hold its head up in fair coverage of the race?

6. *Veracity and Confirmation.* We're getting this information from a source who has been promised anonymity. What steps can we take to confirm the information? It helps that the legally obtained material from the public library seems to corroborate the video list. Ideally, however, if unrealistically, firsthand confirmation would be preferable. Perhaps our anonymous clerk knows that the senator checks out a video every Friday night. Should we emulate the Gary Hart case, when a reporter literally lurked in the bushes, and put someone on the senator's tail? Can we find a source who has attended "video parties" at the senator's home?

7. *The Internet Connection.* The video information has been sent to our reporter, and "a dozen or so others," on Internet. The communications highway is full of potholes. Any self-respecting computer hacker can break into e-mail. Does this mean the information is no longer "private," and that we're just relaying what is already available to the public? What perils do we face from relying on Internet-sourced information?

8. *The Senator's Persona.* I don't think we can disregard the senator himself in our decision making. Does the man have a history of pedophillia or any other sex-related offenses? At the other end of the spectrum, is he an outspoken purveyor of censorship and moral rectitude? Either extreme might help justify a decision to run the story. The former would bolster the

public's need to know that the man poses a threat; the latter would show him to be a raving hypocrite.

9. *How Will We Play the Story*? Okay, say we've considered all of the issues and decide to run with the story. How will we present it? Banner headline, down-page or inside story, simply reporting that this information came from a reliable source? Would we run it without a comment from the senator, or even just "no comment," provided he was given ample time to respond?

We'll never answer all of these questions but we do need to raise as many as possible. The senator's credibility and respectability may be on the line, but so are the newspaper's.

By Lynn Feigenbaum
Public Editor
The Virginian-Pilot and *The Ledger-Star*
Norfolk, VA

Commentary #2

A Time for "Show and Tell"?

The media have made Americans into a nation of "peeping Toms." In refusing to draw lines about what information is essential to the public interest and what is mere curiosity about the rich and famous, the press (print and broadcast) has also catered to the public's, and its own, baser instincts. It loses on both counts.

"Show and tell" used to be an activity for kindergartners. Today, it ranks high on the list of what the media do best. Millions of Americans glued themselves to the television tube during the "slow chase" of O. J. Simpson on Los Angeles freeways. Millions watched the rape trial of William Kennedy Smith, and millions more learned the name of his accuser after one Florida tabloid printed it.

Technology has helped to change the way we evaluate individual privacy rights. It not only allows accidents and crimes and other compelling events of our lives into our homes even as they happen, but fosters the sense that if the media do not fully report everything they are capable of finding out, they are delinquent in fulfilling their mission of "informing the public." Competition increases compulsion to report. If one television station has footage, or a newspaper has a story and a photo, the others are driven to match or to go one better.

Lines that once might have been drawn by individual members of the media have been washed out by what is now possible to find out. The result is that now decisions to publish are, in effect, made in somebody else's newsroom.

The media have created a public taste for information people once found distasteful. Even as ordinary citizens declare themselves sick of what's on the menu, they continue to stuff themselves with what is seamy and slimy.

They suppress the abiding fear that should they ever become involved in an accident, or a crime, or choose to put themselves in positions of leadership, they will get the same cavalier treatment they have seen given to others.

There are vast differences in the privacy accorded public figures and that ceded to private persons. Public figures, whether politicians or actresses or sports heroes, are considered to have forfeited most of their personal privacy by virtue of earning a living out of the public pocket or holding themselves up as leaders.

Ordinary people know that the media ignore what's in their garbage cans, what books they read, and what videos they watch, or what happens in their bedrooms, because they simply do not care. People love the press for taking them to its peep show, and fear it for its capacity to make them part of the act.

The U.S. Constitution guarantees us no explicit privacy rights. With some exceptions, privacy is an evolving concept in the law, and the press mostly deals with it on a case-by-case basis. It draws its lines in the shifting sands.

The confirmation hearings of Robert Bork for the U.S. Supreme Court a few years ago resulted in new—albeit limited—barriers to the media barging in on people's personal lives, even when those persons are nominees for the Supreme Court. Congress passed what has come to be known as the "Bork Bill" when, during the hearings, a Washington, DC weekly paper published the titles of tapes Bork had rented. The list of titles was provided by a television/videotape rental store.

Angry senators responded with a law (The Video Privacy Protection Act, 18 U.S.C. § 2710, 1988) that prevented the unauthorized release of specific titles rented by identifiable individuals.

The law is probably no more than a Band-Aid on the gush of information about individuals that new technology is sending down the public pipeline. Almost nothing is sacred or insulated from the gaze of the voyeurs we have all become. We have a press that often uses information without thought to whether it has value to the public interest (as opposed to public curiosity).

Has the right to publish become the mandate to publish?

When you, as an editor, receive a list of videos rented by an incumbent senator running for reelection and a list of books the senator borrowed from the library, how do you decide whether the information is of vital public interest or merely caters to its penchant for voyeurism?

The video list, whose titles and topics raise suspicion about the senator's character, was on Internet, so you know your competitors probably have it too. Is that a factor in your decision to publish? Does it matter what the senator watches or reads so long as there is no evidence that it has prompted any action on his part? Is it conceivable that a person helping to create laws affecting behavior and safeguarding values might want to know what threatens those values? Does it matter if that politician has presented himself to voters as an honorable and decent individual who stands for the highest level of morality and probity? Does the list reveal an ongoing interest in smarmy or violent activity, an obsession with aberrant sexual behavior, or merely a normal curiosity about what constituents may be viewing and reading?

In a society as obsessed with sex as ours is, do we want leaders to make value judgments based on hearsay or from knowing what these materials actually contain? Finally, in the absence of any behavior by the senator linked to such reading and viewing materials, should he be held up to public criticism for doing precisely what other citizens do at no risk to their reputations? Should public officials be held to a higher standard?

All of these questions should be asked and answered before a decision is made about making the lists public. Once answered, they should be weighed for their significance to the public interest. If those answers favor publication, it should be done—without apology. If they do not, the lists should be discarded—without apology. Ethical journalism requires drawing lines that cannot be washed away by the tide of lesser standards.

By Jean Otto
Reader Representative
Rocky Mountain News
Denver, CO

Commentary #3

Politics and Privacy

Political journalists face the difficult task of sifting through voluminous data about candidates and selecting the information voters need to cast thoughtful ballots. In most cases, that information includes more than simply voting records and stances on political, economic, and social issues. It includes facts about character—the personal attributes that help determine a candidate's moral fitness for public office.

To many voters, information about the "person" is more important than a candidate's position on substantive issues. Rumors of adultery and other personal matters lead today's discussions about American politics.

Whether this heightened interest in the personal lives of candidates is due simply to public curiosity or to the media's legitimization of character issues as newsworthy is uncertain. The fact is, however, that media coverage of politicians has become increasingly more intrusive into candidates' private lives. The need to evaluate the ethics of political communication is clear.

Although hearing about a senator watching *Debbie Does Dallas* might be far more titillating (and sell more newspapers) than a discussion of welfare reform, a story about the senator's personal viewing habits cannot be justified on the basis of satisfying public curiosity alone. A greater good must be identified.

Journalists must be careful not to step beyond the bounds of human decency and report private facts that have no relevance to a candidate's ability to perform the duties of the office sought. Many personal matters should remain just that—personal. Private information should not automatically be slated for publication. If there is no public interest involved, people should be left alone.

Individuals suffer tremendous emotional pain and embarrassment when personal matters become front-page headlines. Even politicians deserve sensitive treatment by the media. The public's need to know should be carefully balanced with a respect for individual privacy. Political careers and personal reputations are easily destroyed by unsubstantiated stories that later prove to be false.

This case presents a particularly troubling ethical dilemma for journalists and demonstrates the need for journalistic guidelines regarding the publication of private information about public figures. Just how far should the media go in revealing the personal lives of politicians?

Questions that may help guide the decision-making process in this and similar cases include the following.

First, will the media incur legal liability by publishing the information? Regarding the video rental list, the "Bork Bill" makes no mention of media liability for publishing video rentals. Additionally, the limited case law in this area of privacy suggests that no liability exists in such situations. Of course, until a specific issue is tested in the courts, some doubt remains. Certainly, the spirit of the law might be violated in some cases.

Although invasion of privacy is a legal issue, privacy decisions most often faced by journalists involve not legal but ethical questions. Journalists routinely wrestle with the question: "When is it in the public interest to invade someone's privacy?" Although public figures—and particularly politicians—are afforded less privacy than ordinary people, journalists must still determine when they have strayed beyond the limits of reason. The next questions help define the boundaries.

Second, can the information be verified and documented? In this case, the video rental list has not been authenticated. How does the editor know the list is accurate? An anonymous source via Internet should make one skeptical. If the lists cannot be verified, they should not be published.

Third, is the information directly relevant to the campaign and the official's fitness for office? Does this private information about a political candidate meet the definition of news that consumers need to make informed decisions?

If the information demonstrates disparity between the private and public individual and/or exposes a violation of public trust, then the story warrants further inquiry. If for example, the senator has become known for his crusades against pornography, then his personal viewing habits probably deserve public scrutiny. If he has been outspoken on issues concerning the "religious right," then his reading of materials concerning such issues may be of public interest. Hypocritical behavior, particularly if persistent, is something voters need to know about.

Finally, is the story balanced—has the "accused" been afforded an opportunity to respond? Any explanation should be included as part of the story. It would be unfair to run the story without the senator's comment.

These questions deserve thoughtful consideration by journalists and editors who control the flow of information to the voting public. It is important to keep in mind that it is the voters who should cast the deciding ballots—not the media. The media's role in the electoral process is to deliver the information on which these important decisions are based.

By Kathy R. Fitzpatrick
Assistant Professor, Communications
Southern Methodist University

Commentary #4

The Journalist's Contract

Journalists are hard pressed to find any greater conflict in their professional lives than that between rights to privacy and the need for audiences to have information.

In the case presented, it can be argued forcefully that my effective knowledge as a reader is not significantly enhanced if I know my senator rents strange movies or reads literature espousing a view I find deplorable. At the same time, the senator, if he were concerned about peoples' reactions to his information sources (Who can deny that *Debbie Does Dallas* is information rich?), could well choose to remain ignorant on significant and very controversial issues. In that event, his ability to make decisions affecting us all is likely to be as significantly impaired as is that of the more demagogic of his critics. We would have to assume that right- or left-leaning literature, or books in Russian or Japanese, or Hitler's *Mein Kampf*, or Marx's *Das Kapital*, would be almost as inflammatory to some as pedophillia is to others. He could, of course, send an aide to rent/check out these materials out of his own fear of detection, but such intellectual cowardice is another ethics topic.

It is probably a tragic commentary on the ability of segments of our society to handle information well that such a question even comes up, but the problem is real and in some circumstances public officials and public figures have learned they must be very careful about the images they project.

This caution, of course, may have a profound effect on the reality of their ability to function in office. There are many reasons for any of the contacts the senator has chosen to have with the materials listed, many of them noble: "What is pedophillia?" is not a disingenuous question for many sheltered folk who may need to see what it is that should scandalize them. In that vein, of course, a compelling argument can be made that public officials' privacy should be protected because such disclosures as are mentioned in this case accomplish no good, and privacy allows the public official to search for information without fear of public vengeance, thus producing a better public servant. Certainly, the vote must be to protect privacy by not publishing these materials. Beyond that, of course, privacy is an essential element for quality of life in a democratic society and should be granted if at all justifiable.

On the other hand, profound questions arise about how much a journalist has a moral right to withhold from the public once he or she has information in hand. Having the movie list fall into our laps raises the serious question. Seeking the library list is an affirmative act that places the information in a different perspective.

If the role of the journalist is to service readers/viewers toward informed decisions, it is not out of place to ask the journalist about the nature of his or her contract with those who invest money or time in the product. It is not a difficult stretch for me, as a member of the audience, to tell the journalist: "If you know it, I should know it."

"That," I might argue, "is why I buy/watch you. If you save your best stuff for cocktail parties ('If you only knew what I know!' makes you a hit on the circuit), you are reneging on our contract and trivializing my importance in the social system."

By not publishing the information, journalists deny their audiences the right to make decisions based on full information.

Certainly, full information might be a little much, but we ought not dismiss the concept, for someday it might be important for audiences to know about certain body part sizes, a bit of information public officials can be expected to reluctantly make available. If such an invasion of privacy serves a purpose that discussion may make recognizable or understood, the privacy rights will legitimately be swept aside.

The fact is, I have no idea what information about the senator my audience will find useful, making it important that if I am to err, I should err on the side of disclosure, rather than in the keeping of secrets.

When my time comes to vote and the senator's privacy has been protected, it is a given that I will be voting in some degree (greater or lesser) of ignorance when my media have trivialized my participation in the process by declining to broaden my knowledge of a topic upon which I must make an important decision.

To what degree that ignorance will cripple the social process is difficult to judge, but the proposition that knowledge produces better social decisions than ignorance is very difficult to ignore. It can also be said with some confidence that to institutionalize an overprotection of privacy will profoundly damage the social process.

Society has decided (in the law) that public officials and public figures shall serve as vicarious, visible examples of what most of us normally hold to be private (giving me the ability to observe behavior and its rewards and consequences). This decision, in turn, protects my privacy and that of my neighbor, requiring me to rely on public disclosure of public people. A serious problem, however, is that journalists often do not show me the social process at work by chronicling cause, behavior, and effects, requiring me to piece a great deal together. That, too, is another topic.

We cannot expect a perfect world of disclosure, but overcautious journalists dangerously skew decision-making mechanisms, causing much to become accepted dogma in society out of greater or lesser degrees of ignorance.

Under these terms, journalists have an obligation to publish what they know in order to service the social decision mechanism—in this case, relative to the senator. To withhold the information from the public is to yield to the temptations of comfortable ignorance.

The senator should be prepared for the consequences of his actions, even as he is prepared for the rewards of disclosure of his laudable behavior. His skill in coping with criticism that will come from such disclosures should be an everyday accessory of public life. The journalist is not responsible for making life comfortable for a public official.

Once the viability of both sides is determined, the decision is still there to be made. That decision involves some recognition by the journalist that some information is not useful and that human decency requires a granting of some privacy. I believe I would agree that *Debbie Does Dallas* and the pedophillic material are not relevant, unless the senator has made strong public representations about such materials and such behaviors. In the absence of these representations: (a) such materials can fall within the range of private behaviors allowed a public figure, and/or (b) the latter material can be viewed by the senator in legitimate pursuit of his official duties. (I think I would give him the benefit of the doubt on that one.) The red flag it raises, of course, would alert me to look for future signs.

As to the library materials, I think they (vague as the description is) are not likely to fall into a reasonably protected category, and the senator can legitimately be expected to stand publicly responsible for the act. Indeed, the affirmative act of acquiring the list suggests some sense of newsworthiness on the part of the journalist. A feature story about the senator's reading habits does not unduly invade his privacy; reading materials do not start the emotional hormones racing the same way that movies do. Dealing with the subject matter is something he should be called upon to do publicly, for it appears to fall within a range of political materials that are fair game for the arena.

By Ralph D. Barney
Professor of Communications
Brigham Young University

www.ingramcontent.com/pod-product-compliance
Ingram Content Group UK Ltd.
Pitfield, Milton Keynes, MK11 3LW, UK
UKHW020427010325
455677UK00029B/1040